T0285987

ALSO BY HIRO KANAGAWA

Indian Arm
The Patron Saint of Stanley Park

FORGIVENESS

Hiro Kanagawa

Illustrated by Cindy Mochizuki

Adapted from the memoir *Forgiveness: A Gift From My Grandparents* by Mark Sakamoto

PLAYWRIGHTS CANADA PRESS
TORONTO

Cover and interior art © Cindy Mochizuki
Author photo by Noah Asanias
Illustrator photo by Jessica Jacobson

Playwrights Canada Press
202-269 Richmond St. W., Toronto, ON M5V 1X1
416.703.0013 | info@playwrightscanada.com | www.playwrightscanada.com

For professional or amateur production rights, please contact:
Colin Rivers at Marquis Entertainment
402–10 Adelaide St. East, Toronto, ON M5C 1J3
416-960-9123 x 223 | info@mqlit.ca

LIBRARY AND ARCHIVES CANADA CATALOGUING IN PUBLICATION
Title: Forgiveness / by Hiro Kanagawa ; adapted from the memoir Forgiveness: a gift
   from my grandparents by Mark Sakamoto ; illustrations by Cindy Mochizuki.
Names: Kanagawa, Hiro, 1963- author. | Mochizuki, Cindy, illustrator. | Dramatization of
   (work): Sakamoto, Mark, 1977- Forgiveness.
Description: Includes some text in Japanese.
Identifiers: Canadiana (print) 20220470243 | Canadiana (ebook) 20220470480
   | ISBN 9780369103949 (softcover) | ISBN 9780369103956 (PDF) | ISBN 9780369103963 (EPUB)
Subjects: LCSH: Sakamoto, Mitsue, 1920-—Family—Drama. | LCSH: MacLean, Ralph,
   1922-—Family—Drama. | LCSH: Sakamoto, Mark, 1977-—Family—Drama. | LCSH:
   World War, 1939-1945—Prisoners and prisons, Japanese—Drama. | LCSH: Prisoners
   of war—Canada—Drama. | LCSH: Prisoners of war—Japan—Drama. | CSH: Japanese
   Canadians—Forced relocation and internment, 1941-1949—Drama. | CSH: Japanese
   Canadians—Drama. | LCGFT: Drama. | LCGFT: Biographical drama. | LCGFT: Historical
   drama. | LCGFT: Theatrical adaptations.
Classification: LCC PS8621.A486 F67 2023 | DDC C812/.6—dc23

Playwrights Canada Press operates on land which is the ancestral home of the
Anishinaabe Nations (Ojibwe / Chippewa, Odawa, Potawatomi, Algonquin, Saulteaux,
Nipissing, and Mississauga), the Wendat, and the members of the Haudenosaunee
Confederacy (Mohawk, Oneida, Onondaga, Cayuga, Seneca, and Tuscarora), as well as
Metis and Inuit peoples. It always was and always will be Indigenous land.

We acknowledge the financial support of the Canada Council for the Arts, the Ontario
Arts Council (OAC), Ontario Creates, and the Government of Canada for our publishing
activities.

 Canada Council   Conseil des arts
for the Arts   du Canada

 ONTARIO ARTS COUNCIL
CONSEIL DES ARTS DE L'ONTARIO
an Ontario government agency
un organisme du gouvernement de l'Ontario

 Canada

 ONTARIO CREATES | ONTARIO CRÉATIF

Dedicated to the memory of
Mitsue Sakamoto and Ralph MacLean.

FOREWORD
MARK SAKAMOTO

Hiro Kanagawa reached out to me in the spring of 2018. He had a big ask: Would I consider assigning the theatrical rights of my book, *Forgiveness: A Gift From My Grandparents* to him? Entrusting someone to bring Mitsue, Ralph, and much of my extended family to life on stage was a giant leap of faith for me to take. I was—to say the very least—cautious. I asked him to break bread with me. I wanted to kick his tires. Hiro accepted and flew from Vancouver to Toronto. My wife Jade and I made miso soup, ohitashi, tsukemono, and teriyaki salmon. We invited Joy Kogawa as a third set of (watchful) eyes. In a few short hours, I knew my ancestors would be in fine hands with Hiro. He was open, deliberate, caring, and, above all, wise. Yet, I asked him for more. Could he please also meet with Ralph, my brother Daniel, and my father Stanley? Unanimously positive reports from them sealed the deal for me. Hiro was off to the races, as they say.

Hiro took his research seriously. He painstakingly walked our family farm outside of Medicine Hat, Alberta. He touched the soil Hideo and Mitsue tilled. He sat with my grandpa Ralph in Calgary, taking meticulous notes. Always feeling more than thinking. Hiro did a wondrous thing—he took my family into his heart. I know he did. I read it on the pages he shared with me. It is quite an honour to have another artist improve upon your work. It is rather surreal when that work is based on the lives of those you love the most. Hiro, in partnership with director Stafford Arima, has taken the people who occupy the whole of my heart and turned them into characters on the stage for all to revel in. It will be surreal to sit beside my dad, Stanley Gene Sakamoto, as his character steps on to the stage. What a beautiful thing! I think I'll hold his hand and cry.

I believe that this theatrical performance transcends entertainment. *Forgiveness* began as a family memoir but has, unfortunately, turned into a warning siren. The forces of nationalism, nativism, and racial discrimination seem to ebb and flow throughout history. There was a perfect storm of all three in the 1940s that brought both sides of my family to their knees. Hate came for my family members. Save their dignity, it took everything from them. They survived those most injurious of years through sheer faith that brighter days were upon them. Somehow, in the depths of their despair, they concluded that the only way out of the hell they were living was to open their hearts. They knew the only way they'd be defeated was if they passed on to their children the transgressions that were committed against them. They refused to bequeath darkness of heart to their children. They used forgiveness as a path forward for them and those that would come after them. I am unspeakably grateful that they did—for I came after them. As you'll see in these pages, those acts of forgiveness on both sides of my family paved the way for the lives of every member of my family. Alas, do we feel those vile forces gathering once again?

Writing the book that this play draws from showed me how much more forgiveness I needed in my own heart. I'd venture a guess and say the same is true of you, too. It is my genuine hope that watching Hiro and Stafford's portrayal of Mitsue Sakamoto and Ralph MacLean illuminates a path for you. I simply cannot wait for the curtains to rise on this heartfelt journey. I hope it leads you to the place you need to be. I am certain that it will remind me of the path I need to be on.

A lawyer by training, Mark Sakamoto has enjoyed a rich and varied career, having worked at a national law firm, a national broadcaster, and served as a senior political advisor to a national party leader. He is Executive Vice President of Think Research, a leading global digital health company with over five hundred employees operating on four continents. In 2014, Mark authored his first book, Forgiveness: A Gift From My Grandparents, *which went on to be a #1 national bestseller, winning CBC Canada Reads in 2018, and hitting #1 again for a second time. In 2020, Mark hosted and was an executive producer on* Good People, *a five-part documentary series that explores humanity's biggest problems, co-produced by Vice Media and CBC. He lives in Toronto and Prince Edward County with his wife and their two daughters.*

PLAYWRIGHT'S NOTES

Forgiveness is my second consecutive adaptation, following on the heels of *Indian Arm* (a modern reinterpretation of Henrik Ibsen's *Little Eyolf*). This is not by design or conscious choice—things just worked out that way. And even if I was writing an original work or something based on my own life experience, to some extent it's *all* adaptation. You may have an idea of the story you want to tell, the characters you want to bring to life, and the play you wind up writing is an adaptation of that idealized vision you have in your head.

The main difference with adapting an existing work is that one feels a keen sense of responsibility—a responsibility not only to the original work and author, but also to those for whom the original occupies a beloved place. *Forgiveness*, the 2018 Canada Reads winner, is surely beloved by countless Canadians, many of whom may have deep personal connections to one of the two central events of the book: the immense losses suffered by Canadian soldiers during the fall of Hong Kong at the beginning of the Pacific War and the subsequent forced removal of Japanese Canadians from the BC coast. *Forgiveness* is also a family memoir about author Mark Sakamoto's actual grandparents, and many of the people we meet in the book are alive and well and eagerly waiting to see how they and their loved ones will be represented on stage. As a playwright, I have to weigh all of the above with yet one more responsibility: my responsibility to write a good play.

It is at this point that you have to give yourself permission to diverge from the original work. Because the original work is not necessarily a good contemporary play—it is not necessarily a play at all. What I've come to learn is that to have a chance at being successful, an adaptation is less a greatest hits playlist of famous scenes and favourite moments and more a reinterpretation of the original's emotional truths. In this sense, my adaptation of *Forgiveness*—like my adaptation of *Little Eyolf*—is not a faithful, note-for-note cover of the original, but it does, I hope, capture the emotional core of what made Mark's book so powerful in the first place: the love of home and family, the faith in human goodness, the courage to fight for what is right, the grace to forgive.

As the Arts Club/Theatre Calgary premiere of *Forgiveness* approaches, I realize that the story of Mitsue Sakamoto and Ralph MacLean is about to undergo yet another profound adaptation, this time by the director, designers, and actors. They will prepare the play for a live audience who, in turn, will interpret the story and characters as they see fit, often in wonderful and unexpected ways. In the theatre it is *all* adaptation, every night, every performance. I cannot wait for that part of the journey to begin.

Forgiveness was adapted for the stage by permission of Mark Sakamoto and Westwood Creative Artists (Michael Levine/Caroline Vassallo). The play was originally commissioned by the Arts Club Theatre Company (Vancouver, British Columbia) and Theatre Calgary (Calgary, Alberta). Additional development support was provided by the 2019 Banff Playwrights Lab and the National Creation Fund. *Forgiveness* was first produced by the Arts Club Theatre Company and Theatre Calgary and premiered in January 2023 at both theatres with the following cast and creative team:

Mitsue: Yoshie Bancroft
Miyoko, Mrs. Yamamoto, and Hong Kong Woman: June Fukumura
Tomi and Launderer's Wife: Manami Hara
Hideo: Kevin Takahide Lee
Yosuke, Kato, and Launderer: Jovanni Sy
Stan and Pat: Daniel Fong
Ron, the Suitors, and Ichiro: Isaac Li
Ralph: Griffin Cork
Deighton, Adams, and Police Officer (Wedding): Jacob Leonard
Cooper and Police Officer (Hastings): Fionn Laird
Ralph's Father, Recruiter, Mortimer, and Mr. Archibald: Jerod Blake
Phyllis, Ralph's Mother, Darlene, and Mrs. Rutt: Alana Hawley Purvis
Diane, Dress Shop Socialite, Nurse, and Woman On Train: Allison Lynch

Director: Stafford Arima
Assistant Director: Howard Dai
Dramaturg: Stephen Drover
Set Design: Pam Johnson
Lighting Design: John Webber
Sound Design: Joshua Reid
Costume Design: Joanna Yu
Video and Animation Design: Cindy Mochizuki

Video Systems Design: Sammy Chien and Chimerik Collective
(Kayleigh Sandomirsky and Caroline MacCaull)
Composer: Reza Jacobs
Stage Manager: Erika Morey
Assistant Stage Manager: Peter Jotkus
Apprentice Stage Manager: Evan Ren
Cultural Consultant, Japanese Canadian Dialect and Experience:
Julie Tamiko Manning
East Coast Canadian Dialect: Jane MacFarlane
Japanese Language Coach: Yayoi Hirano

CAST

The cast of thirteen consists of three Asian women, four Asian men, four white men, and two white women. In addition to the main characters below, most of the cast will play multiple characters as indicated.

The vast majority of the "men" who fought in the battles depicted were barely twenty. Best efforts should be made to cast actors in their late teens to very early twenties to play the Canadian and Japanese soldiers.

Asterisk (*): voice only

Double asterisk (**): non-speaking

Actor	Character(s)
1. Asian woman, plays a character from their teens to their late forties (some Japanese dialogue)	Mitsue
2. Asian woman, plays characters from their teens to their late forties (significant Japanese dialogue)	Miyoko, Mrs. Yamamoto, and Hong Kong Woman**
3. Older Asian woman, plays characters from their late thirties to their sixties (significant Japanese dialogue)	Tomi and Launderer's Wife**

4. Asian man, plays characters from their early twenties to their late forties (significant Japanese dialogue)	Hideo
5. Older Asian man, plays characters from their thirties to their sixties (significant Japanese dialogue)	Yosuke, Kato, and Launderer
6. Younger Asian man, plays characters from their childhood to their twenties (a few words of Japanese)	Stan and Pat
7. Younger Asian man, plays characters from their childhood to their twenties (a few words of Japanese)	Ron, the Suitors, and Ichiro
8. White man, plays a character from their childhood to their late forties (a few words of Japanese)	Ralph
9. White man, plays characters from their childhood to their twenties	Deighton, Adams, and Police Officer (Wedding)
10. White man, plays characters from their childhood to their thirties	Cooper and Police Officer (Hastings)
11. Older white man, plays characters from their forties to their sixties	Ralph's Father, Recruiter, Mortimer, and Mr. Archibald

12. White woman, plays characters from their teens to their forties	Phyllis, Ralph's Mother, Darlene, and Mrs. Rutt
13. White woman, plays characters from their teens to their forties	Diane, Dress Shop Socialite, Nurse, and Woman On Train
Radio Voices	Radio Nanking,* Radio Honolulu,* Radio Hong Kong,* CBC Radio,* and Winston Churchill*
Additionally, the cast above populate the stage as:	Pedestrians, Protesters, Bus Passengers, Soldiers, Guards, and POWS

MAIN AND SUPPORTING CHARACTERS

JAPANESE

MITSUE: *Nisei* woman in her teens to late forties. Full of hope and dreams. She possesses inherent goodness and grace and lives as if these things matter. If she has a fault, it is a fierce clarity about what is right. Though she surely raised her voice in anger from time to time, it is said of her today that no one once ever heard her do it.

HIDEO: *Nisei* man in his twenties to late forties. Educated and progressive, but speaks with an accent, having been sent back to Japan as a child. Adores Mitsue but is disillusioned by the internment.

STAN: *Sansei* man in his childhood to his twenties. Mitsue and Hideo's second son. A "people person," he has inherited his mother's innate goodness.

RON: *Sansei* man in his childhood to his twenties. Mitsue and Hideo's eldest son. A Japanese Canadian Prairie boy with dreams of hockey and rock and roll.

KATO: Japanese POW camp commandant in his thirties. Arrogant and sadistic but believes himself to be a worldly and educated man.

PAT: *Nisei* man. Mitsue's brother. Wants to be accepted as fully Canadian and bristles at his own Japaneseness.

YOSUKE AND TOMI: *Issei* couple in their late forties to sixties. Mitsue's parents. They aspire to middle-class respectability in Canada for themselves and assimilation for their children.

ICHIRO: *Nisei* man in his twenties. Until Hideo, Mitsue's most serious suitor. He dreams of a fully assimilated life in Canada for himself and Mitsue, but his idealism is shattered by the internment.

MIYOKO: *Nisei* girl in her teens. Mitsue's best friend. Trying to be a typical Canadian teen despite having a strict Japanese father.

MRS. YAMAMOTO: *Issei* woman in her late thirties to forties. Kindly dress shop owner and would-be matchmaker to Mitsue and Hideo.

WHITE

RALPH: Grindstone boy in his childhood to early twenties. Like Mitsue, he has an innate sense of morality and fairness and continues to believe in these things through the horrors of war. Signs up for war in search of escape from a small and abusive life at home. Spends the rest of his life searching for the meaning of his suffering.

DEIGHTON: Grindstone boy in his childhood to early twenties. Ralph's best friend. Naive, good-time Charlie.

COOPER: Grindstone boy in his childhood to early twenties. Ralph and Deighton's friend. Coarser, more crudely male.

PHYLLIS: Ralph's long-suffering wife, in her forties. Trying her best to support Ralph through his PTSD. Trying her best not to disapprove of her daughter dating a Japanese Canadian.

DIANE: A Prairie girl in her twenties. Ralph's daughter. Not a hippie, not a rebel, just happened to fall in love with a Japanese guy.

MORTIMER: A Canadian officer from the stiff-upper-lip military academy. In his thirties. He does his best to keep himself and Ralph alive.

ADAMS: A straight-talking Marine in his twenties. Has probably seen horrible things that only Americans fighting in the Pacific will ever see.

MRS. RUTT: Sugar beet farmer, middle-aged. Not consciously cruel or racist, but entirely comfortable with housing a Japanese family in a chicken coop.

MR. ARCHIBALD: A tailor who Mrs. Yamamoto entrusts with valuable items from her dress shop and who later takes her shop over.

SET

There is an evocation of dirt. The dirt is at times a beet farm in Alberta, a battlefield or POW camp in Hong Kong or Japan, the dusty roads of the Magdalen Islands and Celtic, BC, etc.

There are crude wooden structures that evoke the interior and exterior spaces of prison camps, livestock stalls, chicken coops, and modest working-class homes.

Props and decor to create Mitsue's kitchen and other interiors are taken from the crates and trunks as needed and packed away again at a moment's notice.

The back of the stage requires a cyclorama or equivalent for lighting effects and projections.

TIME

The "present" of the play is the spring of 1968 as Mitsue and Ralph prepare to meet one another for dinner at her home. The play inter-cuts between this present and their various experiences before, during, and after World War II.

PROPOSED PROJECTIONS

I imagine a heavy usage of projected animation and imagery. These visuals evoke Japanese *sumi-e* and *manga*, the graininess of archival photos and newsreels, the scratchy pen and charcoal drawings made by soldiers and POWs, etc. I intend for the projected imagery to unify the piece visually and provide a more expressionistic, intentional aesthetic than, say, projecting a mishmash of imagery from a variety of media.

I also hope the projected imagery, like all theatre lighting, can be used to evoke space. The spaces in this play range from the vastness of Prairie beet fields to the enclosed bilge of a Japanese hell ship to the utter chaos of a battlefield.

PRONUNCIATIONS

Mitsue: Me-tsoo-eh
Hideo: He-day-oh
Yosuke: Yo-skeh
Celtic: Sel-tick
Shamshuipo: Sham-shwee-poe
Niigata: Nee-ga-ta
Kato: Kah-toe

ACT I

PROLOGUE

An empty sky. An empty landscape. Two Japanese women appear, dressed in their 1940s Sunday best, struggling to carry suitcases and scant belongings: MITSUE *and her mother* TOMI. *An* POLICE OFFICER *watches over them.*

On the opposite side of the stage, a JAPANESE GUARD *marches in three Canadian* POWS: RALPH, COOPER, *and their commanding officer* MORTIMER. *The prisoners are exhausted, on the verge of collapse.*

POLICE OFFICER: Keep it moving, ladies!

JAPANESE GUARD: *ARUKE! [WALK!]*

TOMI: *Nante hidoi koto . . . [How horrible . . .]*

RALPH: Jeezus, I'm cramping bad . . .

COOPER moans in agony.

TOMI: This is the horse arena. *Mitsue, oboeteru? [Mitsue, remember?]* We saw a horse show here at PNE.

MITSUE: Mama, *shinpai shinaide [don't worry]*, it's just for registration.

MORTIMER: Hang on, boys. The camp's around the bend. We're almost there.

RALPH: You said that ten miles ago.

RALPH is struggling badly.

Oh God . . . Goddammit . . .

COOPER: I can't anymore . . . I can't.

MORTIMER: Tough it out. Do it. You gotta stand straight and walk. Come on now.

TOMI sees where they are being led.

TOMI: *Masaka. Chikusha? [It can't be. Livestock stalls?]* These pens are for cows and pigs.

MITSUE: They're just . . . they're just holding us here. Then we'll be on our way.

TOMI: Where?

MITSUE: I don't know.

TOMI: *Ittai doyu koto? [What is this nonsense?]*

MITSUE: Mama, I don't know.

RALPH: I gotta rest. I gotta.

MORTIMER: No. No. Keep moving. Stay up.

RALPH: Are they gonna shoot me? Don't let 'em shoot me, Captain . . .

MORTIMER: Move your feet, MacLean! Come on now! Don't you go down!

RALPH groans, falters. TOMI is stunned at the sight of animal filth on the ground.

TOMI: They didn't even clean for us.

MITSUE: *Mama, shikkari shite. [Mama, be strong.]* Let's hold our heads high.

POLICE OFFICER: Hey! Get a move on!

The GUARD prods MITSUE with his baton.

MITSUE: Don't you dare!

POLICE OFFICER: What did you say to me?

MITSUE: How dare you poke at me with your stick! Like some animal?

POLICE OFFICER: Lady, I'm warning you.

MITSUE: Where are our families? Our men? Where are our husbands!

POLICE OFFICER: Shut up, you!

RALPH doubles over.

JAPANESE GUARD: *ARUKE HORA! [WALK GODDAMMIT!]*

MITSUE: Listen to me, please—

TOMI: Mitsue! *Yamenasai!* [*Stop!*]

MORTIMER: MacLean! Get up! MacLean! No . . . !

The POLICE OFFICER raises his baton menacingly. The JAPANESE GUARD brings his bayonet up to spearing position.

Title: Forgiveness: A Gift From My Grandparents.

Animation: An evocation of geographical place and cultural space: Lower Mainland, BC, Canada, and Japan.

*MITSUE and RALPH drift down stage to address the audience as
other actors unpack crates and boxes and assemble what will
serve as various interior spaces throughout the act: MITSUE's
kitchen, the Oseki and MacLean homes, MRS. YAMAMOTO's
dress shop, etc.*

MITSUE & RALPH: Hello.

MITSUE: I'm Mitsue.

RALPH: Ralph. Ralph Augustus MacLean.

MITSUE: Mitsue Margaret Sakamoto, née Oseki. I was born in 1920, in Eburne, BC, a little town on Sea Island just across the Fraser from Vancouver. You know that fancy shopping mall on the way to the airport? That was Eburne.

RALPH: I was born in 1922, about as far from there as you could get. Grindstone, Magdalen Islands, Quebec. Basically a pile of rocks in the Gulf of St. Lawrence, but the hardest, most rugged, most beautiful pile of rocks you ever did see. Same goes for the people.

MITSUE: We moved across the river to Vancouver after I was born. To Celtic Cannery in the Southlands at the foot of Balaclava. It was a neighbourhood of . . . oh . . . twenty-five or so Japanese families. Fishermen mostly, but we had our own church, a little store, a Japanese school. It was home. Our happy, beloved, Canadian home . . .

RALPH: Home. Never lived there after the war, but I'll always be a Grindstone boy, and proud of it. Per capita, the Magdalen Islands probably sent more men—more boys—to the war than anywhere else in Canada. Most of 'em never did make it back.

MITSUE: It's said the scars of war, the hurt, the pain, get passed down through generations. Some scars never heal.

RALPH: But you learn to live with 'em. You learn to live.

MITSUE: This is our story. But it's also yours.

RALPH: So, welcome. I'm not much of a host but Mitsue here sure is. I'll see ya in a bit.

He exits. MITSUE heads for her kitchen.

MITSUE: Come on in then. *Dozo ohairi kudasai. [Please come in.]*

She puts on a pair of glasses, stoops a little from twenty-five years of relentless work and . . .

Animation: transition to MITSUE's home in Medicine Hat.

Title: Medicine Hat, Alberta. August 1968.

MITSUE, now twenty-five years older, bustles about in the small kitchen. Her husband, HIDEO, sits with a bowl of rice and okazu [sides], having just returned from work. Their son, STAN, in his early twenties, enters.

STAN: *Tadaima. [I'm home.]*

MITSUE & HIDEO: *Hai, okairi. [Yes, welcome back.]*

HIDEO goes back to eating. MITSUE continues to bustle.

STAN: Mom, what are you doing? It's midnight.

MITSUE: Your wheeler-dealer brother is bringing one of his rock-and-roll bands over.

STAN: Which one?

MITSUE: Guess Who?

STAN: I don't know.

MITSUE: It's a band Ronnie's promoting. He said they're pretty famous.

STAN: Well who are they?

MITSUE: He said Guess Who.

STAN: I don't know, Mom.

MITSUE: Well I thought that's what he said. Guess Who.

STAN: Wait. *The* Guess Who? *The* Guess Who. Why didn't you say so?

MITSUE: I thought I did.

STAN: Nope.

MITSUE: I don't understand you kids sometimes.

HIDEO grunts assent.

STAN: Well they're big news, Mom—really big. Good for Ron.

MITSUE: Anyway I'm just fixing the boys a little something. I'm sure they'll be hungry.

STAN: Speaking of which, guess who's coming for dinner?

MITSUE: Is this a riddle?

STAN: You know the girl I've been seeing.

MITSUE: Which one?

HIDEO: Guess who!

MITSUE: You have so many friends, Stan, I don't know which ones you're dating.

STAN: Diane. You've met her.

MITSUE: Diane. With the sister Darlene?

STAN: Her cousin Darlene lives here in the Hat. And Diane's parents are coming to visit from Calgary, so I thought we could have them over for dinner.

MITSUE: So it's serious.

STAN: It's just a friendly dinner.

MITSUE: Well I'm sure I can whip something up.

STAN: Great, only thing is, lemme just confirm what they can eat.

MITSUE: Oh. Are they Jewish? Because I've cooked for Jewish people.

STAN: No, no. Diane's dad is a war hero. Ralph MacLean—he was in the paper. He was a POW in Japan. He had it pretty rough over there. I just want to make sure he's okay with Japanese food. Rice and whatnot.

MITSUE: Oh?

STAN: What's wrong?

MITSUE: I don't have to cook Japanese.

STAN: Everybody loves your cooking. Look at all the bands Ron brings home.

MITSUE: Well they're beatniks or hippies or whatever you call them. But a lot of folks are set in their ways and our food is one more thing they want to hold against us. White kids used to tease me— they used to tease you. You begged me not to pack *onigiri* in your lunch. Ronnie got in fights over Japanese food.

STAN: Mom. We're not in sixth grade anymore. And Diane's parents aren't like that.

MITSUE: You brought it up. You want to make a good impression. And you're worried my food will be too Japanese.

STAN: Mom, no. Forget I mentioned it. I'm sure it'll be fine.

MITSUE: Well, let me know.

*HIDEO points to a crate under the counter, partially obscured
by a* noren *[small Japanese curtain].*

HIDEO: *Soiyeba [Now that you mention it]*, Stanley, how much rice
we have?

*STAN and MITSUE exchange a look. STAN slides the crate out. (It
is the box from the* Forgiveness *book cover.)*

STAN: It's like two-thirds full, Dad.

MITSUE: Three-quarters.

STAN: At least three-quarters. Nearly seven-eighths. It's basically full.

HIDEO: I get more tomorrow.

STAN: Dad, there's like thirty, thirty-five pounds in here.

MITSUE: Probably forty.

STAN: Oh yeah.

HIDEO: Okay. Must get more.

HIDEO starts out then stops.

We have toilet paper?

Beat.

I check.

He exits. STAN turns to see MITSUE beaming at him.

STAN: What, Mother?

MITSUE: I'm happy for you. Dating the daughter of a war hero. *Sugoi-janai. [Isn't that wonderful.]* Have some *ocha* and tell me all about them.

We hear the blues-rock strains of the Guess Who circa 1967.

STAN: Me and Diane actually met at one of Ronnie's dance parties.

DIANE and her cousin DARLENE enter on a wave of laughter and good times, showing off their dance moves to one another. RON breezes by, trying hard to look like a mod impresario.

DARLENE: Ronnie! Where's your brother? My cousin came all the way from Calgary and needs a boy to dance with.

DIANE: A good one, too, none of these farm boys.

RON: I'll dance with you. I'm actually much better than my brother.

DARLENE: You dance like a hockey player.

RON: I am a hockey player.

(to DIANE) I could've player Junior A if I was a little taller.

STAN crosses from his scene with MITSUE in the kitchen.

STAN: And learned to skate.

(to DIANE) I skate circles around him. Hi. Stan Sakamoto.

DIANE: Diane MacLean. Nice to . . . Wait. Sak-a-moto? Are you the Hack-a-moto brothers? You're the dirtiest players in Alberta!

RON: Define "dirty."

DIANE: They call you Hack-a-moto.

STAN: I always took it as a compliment. Didn't you, Ron?

RON: Absolutely.

STAN: *(to MITSUE)* Right, Mom?

MITSUE: Hey! Watch number seven! Hit him! Hit him! Don't take any guff from nobody!

> *A new song comes on. DIANE shrieks and busts out the moves. STAN joins in, impressing her. RON and DARLENE also dance. MITSUE beams. After a beat STAN, RON, and the girls head for the kitchen. STAN sits back down as RON and the girls head off.*

Well she sounds like a fun girl.

STAN: She really is, Mom. I can't wait for you to meet her—

RON: *(as he passes through)* Ma, I'm bringing the band by after their gig tonight. They heard about your *gyozas* and *yakisoba*, if you don't mind.

MITSUE: Sure, Ronnie, I got nothing better to do at two a.m.

> *RON and the girls exit, waving. As MITSUE and STAN settle back into their conversation at the table, RALPH appears, twenty-five years older than when we first saw him. He's standing in the middle of his darkened bedroom in an undershirt and trousers. He clutches his head and moves his feet obsessively, struggling with unseen demons.*

And her father, you've met him obviously. He's fair toward you? He doesn't have any hard feelings about the war?

STAN: The war? As in World War II? Nobody cares about that anymore.

RALPH: *Sumimasen . . . Shitsurei-itashimashita . . . [Yes . . . I'm sorry . . . My apologies . . .]*

MITSUE: *Hai . . .* Oh yes we do, Stanley.

STAN: That was twenty-five years ago. Folks are more concerned about Vietnam, civil rights, things going on right now.

RALPH sees STAN and calls out angrily.

RALPH: Hey! I want a word with you.

STAN stands to face RALPH. RALPH stares him down.

Next time I see my daughter on that bike of yours without a helmet—

STAN: I'm sorry, sir, we were just—

RALPH: You're taking her life in your hands. That mean anything to you?

STAN: Yes, sir.

RALPH: Speak up.

STAN: Yes, sir!

RALPH: You're taking her life in your hands.

STAN: You . . . said that already—

RALPH: I know what I said. Does it mean anything to you?

STAN: Yes, sir, it absolutely does.

RALPH raises a finger at STAN, jabs it at him, but doesn't know what else to say so turns away.

MITSUE: But you get along with him?

STAN: Oh yeah. He . . . he likes me. I think. He's a Leafs fan.

MITSUE: Oh, I like *him* already.

STAN: You and hockey. How many nights did you sit right here at this table, listening to the game on the radio, stencilling labels on beer bottles so me and Ron could have skates?

MITSUE: *(waves it off)* Oh . . . It was just as much for me as for you. I wanted to see you boys play.

STAN: Every night there'd be cases of blank bottles in that corner, and in the morning they'd be sitting over there by the door, done. And by the time the river froze we had skates.

MITSUE: A mother's gotta do what a mother's gotta do.

STAN gets up and gives MITSUE a hug.

STAN: Thanks, Mom. I'll let you know about the dinner.

STAN exits. MITSUE sits in reminiscence for a beat as . . .

Animation: Prairie kids circa 1950 play hockey on a frozen pond. Two Japanese boys (RON and STAN) skate up to join them.

MITSUE: GO HACK-A-MOTOS! Don't let anybody push you around out there!

(*to audience*) Those are my boys!

> *Animation: We travel across the country. The 1950s Prairie
> kids morph into 1930s Maritime boys. They are wearing Maple
> Leafs and Blackhawks jerseys of the era.*

VOICES: Ralphie! Yeah yeah yeah! Give 'er! Give 'er! Oooh! Pass
me the puck, Ralphie, I'm open! Whattaya, blind! Hook me again,
you're dead! Judas! Shoot it, Coop! It's in! It was wide by a mile! Was
not! Was, too!

Title: Grindstone, Magdalen Islands, Quebec. Winter 1936.

RALPH *and two of his buddies,* DEIGHTON *and* COOPER, *appear on stage, all wearing Maple Leafs jerseys. They are walking home from their game.*

DEIGHTON: I was open, Ralphie. None of them Downroaders can cover me.

RALPH: I saw ya.

DEIGHTON: Maybe pass me the puck next time.

RALPH: I did. You missed it.

DEIGHTON: You call that a pass? It was ten feet away!

RALPH: You're slower than a pregnant cow.

COOPER: You couldn't hit a pregnant cow.

Guffaws and roughhousing.

So we going to Sumarah's or what?

RALPH: With what money?

DEIGHTON: Mikey'll slip us something.

COOPER: Not if his pa's there. He's got four eyes in the front and two in the back. Cheap Jewish bastard.

RALPH: He got us these jerseys, Coop.

COOPER: Only so we'd let Mikey play.

DEIGHTON: The Sumarah's are Jewish? I thought they were A-rabs.

COOPER: They're cheap, ain't they?

DEIGHTON: I dunno. Are they? I thought we liked Mikey.

COOPER: Hey, hey, look at this, boys.

They've come to a Chinese laundry, the LAUNDERER and his wife working inside.

Look at them Chinamen in there looking all squinty and chinky.

RALPH: China must be pretty rough all right for them to think coming here is a good idea.

COOPER: Hey! Hey, Chinaman! You and your wife are chinks!

COOPER pulls his eyes into slits.

Chinky-chinky Chinaman!

BOYS: Chinky-chinky Chinaman! Chinky-chinky Chinaman!

DEIGHTON: Uh-oh. He's looking this way.

COOPER: How can you tell? Hey, chinky eyes! Over here!

DEIGHTON: Watch yourself. He might know chop suey.

RALPH: Whattaya talking about, bird brain?

DEIGHTON: Chop suey. That's how they fight.

RALPH: Kung fu. Chop suey is the food.

DEIGHTON: Is not. Chop suey! Ah-ya! Chop-chop! Kung fu is the food. I had it in Charlottetown. Kung fu chicken.

COOPER: Coulda been a stray dog, Deighton, or a donkey's ass. Hey, chink! Lookee lookee!

DEIGHTON: Oh Judas, boys—he's coming this way!

The boys scatter as the LAUNDERER comes storming out of his shop with a hot iron in his fist. RALPH and DEIGHTON get tangled up and DEIGHTON goes down. As DEIGHTON scrambles up, the LAUNDERER swings for his head with the iron, barely missing.

RALPH: Hey! Hey! What do you think you're doing?

LAUNDERER: What *you* doing! What doing!

The LAUNDERER gives DEIGHTON a kick in the butt, sending him sprawling again.

RALPH: Take it easy, mister, we're just having fun with ya.

LAUNDERER: Fun? No. *No fun.* We are working. *Working.* This is place for work. My work! You understand?

Beat.

You understand?

RALPH: Yes.

LAUNDERER: So. You. You. Go away!

The LAUNDERER stalks back to his shop. COOPER comes back, whooping and laughing.

COOPER: Hey, chink! Suck my dink!

DEIGHTON: Ho-ly, Coop!

COOPER and DEIGHTON whoop it up, impressed by COOP's audacity. But RALPH is chagrined.

RALPH: Lay off, fellas. He's working.

COOPER: So?

RALPH: So . . . let a man work, I guess. Come on, ya mugs.

RALPH heads off. COOPER and DEIGHTON stare after him for a beat, confused. Then they burst out laughing.

DEIGHTON: You turning mature or something, Ralphie?

COOPER: I can just see it. Ma drags me to church . . .

COOPER & DEIGHTON: . . . and Ralph's the pastor!

RALPH: *(plays along)* Oh my brudders. If I give you a fish, you're hungry tomorrow. If I teach you to fish—

DEIGHTON: Still hungry tomorrow!

They exit, laughing.

Animation: The Japanese Canadian community in Celtic working like the Chinese launderer. Fishing boats on the Fraser River, Japanese fishermen with their hachimaki *casting their nets. The row houses of Celtic, the Japanese women hanging laundry in their tightly packed yards, the men on land hammering, building, everyone working. We come to an idyllic park with a mighty oak at its centre. Japanese children walk by, coming home from school, their version of work.*

Title: Celtic Cannery, Vancouver, BC. Summer 1939.

BOYS' VOICES: Chinese Japanese! Dirty knees, look at these! Chinese Japanese! Dirty knees, look at these!

MITSUE, late teens, is with her best friend, MIYOKO. They settle in under the tree.

MIYOKO: Stupid boys! What do they even mean? Why are our knees dirty?

MITSUE: Because . . . we scrub floors?

MIYOKO: We don't have floors to scrub—we have *tatami*. *Obaachan's* sit on their knees to drink tea—that's it! *Mo! [Uggh!] Soshite sa [And by the way]*, don't you hate it when they pull their eyes like that? Lots of Japanese have perfectly round eyes. Don't you think so?

MITSUE: Never mind, Miyoko.

MIYOKO: I can't help it. I'm not like you. Why doesn't it bother you?

MITSUE: It does. I'm used to a lot worse from my brother, I guess. You'd think he was *hakujin [white]* the way he talks sometimes.

MIYOKO: Well . . . You know, Mits . . . Pat's actually kinda nice.

MITSUE: Pfft.

MIYOKO: Um . . . thing is . . . he . . . kinda sorta asked me out. I mean, he asked me if I'd like to go for a drive with him in his car.

MITSUE: He did not!

MIYOKO: Just in the afternoon. After church. Not after dinner or anything.

MITSUE: You cannot go out with him, Miyoko, I would die. I would die!

MIYOKO: Well . . . I don't get asked out much. If ever. Before. I mean, I'm just not very *kawaii*.

MITSUE: You're *kawaii*. You're so *kawaii*. You're *bijin*. It's just all the boys know your parents are strict. They're afraid of your dad.

MIYOKO: I know. I'm afraid he's going to marry me off. Remember Tamura Asako, first year at Magee? It happened to her.

MITSUE: Nooo!

MIYOKO: She's engaged to some farmer in Japan. She's never met him. Never even seen a picture.

MITSUE: That's positively barbaric. If my parents did that to me, I'd run away.

MIYOKO: They wouldn't—your parents are forward-thinkers. They don't mind you being Canadianized.

MITSUE: Well they've been here nearly thirty years—way longer than they ever lived in Japan.

MIYOKO: My parents are always talking about sending me "home" to get married. I hear them talking about me sometimes, and it's like I have no say in my own future.

MITSUE: Well they can't expect you to just go along with the old ways and be a good little Japanese girl. Why did they come here in the first place and raise you here? So you could be free and have a good life and be Canadian.

MIYOKO: I suppose. It's so hard being Japanese, *ne*?

MITSUE: If either one of us gets married off against our will, we'll run away together. Promise?

MIYOKO: Promise. Let's just do it anyway.

MITSUE: Let's. We'll be modern Canadian women, you and me.

MIYOKO: I'll be a nurse.

MITSUE: I'll teach school.

MIYOKO: Where would we live?

MITSUE: The West End.

MIYOKO: Mitsue Oseki! We cannot live in the West End. We're not tramps. Our parents would die of shame. Mine would anyway. Yours would be pretty upset, too, and sooner or later you'd have to come back to Celtic.

MITSUE: Why?

MIYOKO: Well to get married and start a family.

MITSUE: What if you met a dreamy young doctor from Shaughnessy? An absolute dreamboat. With soft wavy hair and the most adorable cowlick falling over his brow.

MIYOKO: Tall. With a square jaw. And a very distinguished nose.

MITSUE: What colour eyes?

MIYOKO: Who cares as long as they're not black. It's so boring being Japanese. Why do we all have to be the same? Why can't we have all different kinds of hair and different coloured eyes like *hakujin*? It isn't fair! *Ne*?

A beat. She's struck a nerve.

Mits?

MITSUE: Uh-huh.

MIYOKO: Would you ever?

MITSUE: What?

MIYOKO: Would you ever marry a *hakujin*?

MITSUE: Um . . . Yes?

MIYOKO is scandalized, but in a deliciously thrilling way.

Well why not if we love each other—that's what matters.

MIYOKO: I just . . . I can't see myself. I can't imagine it. It's like picturing myself flying an airplane or doing surgery. It doesn't seem possible. Even if you loved each other, you'd be so alone.

MITSUE: I'd have you. And you'd have me.

Through some mysterious telepathy of friendship they break into a patty-cake routine.

MITSUE & MIYOKO: I met my boyfriend at the candy shop
He bought me ice cream, he bought me cake
He brought me home with a bellyache
Doctor, Doctor, will I die?
Count to five and stay alive
One two three four five . . .
I'M ALIVE!

*Their bliss is interrupted by the entrance of a group of white
protestors carrying picket signs that read "WHITE CANADA" and
"CITIZENS FOR A JAP-FREE BC."*

PROTESTORS: Put the squeeze on the Japanese! Japs out of my BC!
Japs, Japs go on home! Leave my Canada alone!

MITSUE: This is our neighbourhood! *You* go home!

MIYOKO: And it's not even yours! The Musqueam Reserve is down
the street. You stole it from them!

*The girls march off, proud they stood up for themselves. As
the protestors exit, chanting and waving their picket signs,
drunken, victorious Japanese soldiers enter opposite with the
Imperial red ray "rising sun" flag. They pass a bottle among
themselves and terrorize an elderly Chinese prisoner.*

Animation: the spectre of the Imperial Japanese Army in Asia.

RADIO: On this New Year's Day, 1938, the Japanese Army is report-
ing that it has successfully occupied the Chinese city of Nanking,
four months after hostilities began. A Japanese occupation spokes-
man declared that the capture of Nanking represents the fall of "the
main impediment to peace in East Asia . . . "

JAPANESE SOLDIERS: *Tenno-heika, banzai! Banzai! Banzai! [Long live
the emperor!]*

*They hustle their prisoner off. A Japanese soldier takes a swig
from a bottle as he exits and . . .*

SCENE 4

RALPH in his Maple Leafs jersey and his terrified MOTHER *confront the menace of* RALPH's *drunken* FATHER, *who empties a bottle of his own.* RALPH's MOTHER *is on the verge of tears, clutching a rolling pin for dear life.*

MOTHER: You're starving us. You and your bottle. I've got eight children to feed. *Your* children. Crying to be fed. Where is the money for their food, Father? What have you done with the money?

FATHER: Money. Money-money-money. Filthy lucre. Is that all you care about?

He sees RALPH.

More to life, eh, boy?

RALPH's FATHER *laughs.*

Come here.

He staggers over to a phonograph and manages to put on some jaunty music. He starts dancing and is remarkably good.

Come here. Dance, boy!

MOTHER: Leave him be. Go back to your bottle and leave us—

FATHER: DANCE! I said dance, goddammit!

RALPH *tries to shake his legs a little.*

What in hell. Are you mocking me?

RALPH: No, sir.

FATHER: That is pitiful. That is an eyesore. You call that dancing?

RALPH: I'm doing my best. See? I am. I'm dancing . . . I'm dancing—

FATHER: (*throws* RALPH *down*) Dance, goddammit!

MOTHER: STOP IT!

> *She tries to grab* FATHER *but he flings her off. He turns on* RALPH *and kicks him. And again.* RALPH *tries to scuttle away as his father unleashes a barrage of punishment.*

FATHER: You call yourself a MacLean? You dance, boy. That's what we do. MacLean's dance! Are you a son of mine?

(*to* MOTHER) Is this sorry sack of shit you whelped a son of mine? If he's a son of mine, why don't he dance?

> *He returns to kicking* RALPH *again and again.*

You dance, goddammit! Prove yourself! Dance, boy! Dance! Dance!

> *His exertion brings on a coughing fit. He collapses in a chair.* MOTHER *cowers against a wall.* RALPH *is choking and blubbering on the ground.*

Quit crying. The both of yous. Get me my supper, Mutter.

> RALPH *struggles to his feet and staggers out the door.*

MOTHER: Ralph—!

Animation: Under moonlight we see the boy run toward the edge of a cliff, the dark sea crashing far below. As the boy runs, he becomes a teenager, then a youth on the verge of manhood. A second youth joins the first and . . .

DEIGHTON approaches RALPH, sees that he is weeping bitterly, and proceeds with caution.

DEIGHTON: Ralphie? Come away from there, will ya? Quit playing. Step away now.

RALPH: I can't wait to get off this rock, Deighton.

DEIGHTON: I'm with you. Your old man's a tough bastard, all right. Mine, too. So. What say we leave this place, eh? We'll see the world, Ralphie. We'll be men of the world.

RALPH: You're fisherfolk, Deighton. You can sail away any time you want. Me, I'm just dirt and mud and stone. Grindstone. Nothin'.

DEIGHTON: Tell ya what. Come down to the hospital with me in the morning.

RALPH: Aiming to put me in the nut house?

DEIGHTON: Some army chaps are gonna be there. They're recruiting.

RALPH: Recruiting? Tried that already. Wouldn't take me.

DEIGHTON: Whattaya talking about? You tried to enlist? Without me? When was this?

RALPH: Couple months ago. Halifax. When I was visiting my auntie. Saw the office, walked in, asked the man where I could sign up. Said the Army's only taking Prairie boys right now. Prairie boys! Why you got a office in Halifax if you're only taking Prairie boys?

DEIGHTON: Well now they're looking to fill two regiments from just around these parts. Coop's coming, too, unless he gets cold feet.

RALPH: (*wheels turning*) Recruiters? Right here on Grindstone . . .

DEIGHTON: Whattaya think, eh? Worth a look-see.

They take each other in, then shake on it.

RALPH: If you're going, count me in, brudder.

DEIGHTON: Brudder. But tell ya what, Ralphie. You're one royal a-hole for trying to enlist without me. I oughta spit in your eye!

RALPH: You couldn't hit it with a straw. How you gonna shoot a rifle?

DEIGHTON: I'll shoot with my eyes open at least, ya pantywaist.

RALPH: You calling me a pantywaist—that's a laugh!

They cross to the recruiting office and meet up with COOPER. The RECRUITER checks DEIGHTON and COOPER off and waves them through. Jubilant, they wait for RALPH.

RECRUITER: Name.

RALPH: Ralph Augustus MacLean.

RECRUITER: You a Grindstone boy?

RALPH: Yesssir, born and raised.

RECRUITER: How old are you?

RALPH: Eighteen, sir.

A beat.

Eighteen . . . and two months. I was born June 27, 1922.

RECRUITER: Son, you can't go overseas until you're nineteen.

RALPH: I'm fit to serve, sir. I want to fight.

RECRUITER: I don't doubt that, but I got my orders.

> *RALPH exchanges an anguished look with DEIGHTON and*
> *COOPER. Then:*

RALPH: Wait a minute . . . what am I thinking? I was born . . . same year as them. That's right, sir. I was born June 27, *1921.*

RECRUITER: *(entering the date)* Nineteen . . . *twenty-one.* That's more like it. All right, then. Welcome to the Royal Rifles, soldier.

> *RALPH joins the others and they celebrate.*

DEIGHTON: Royal Rifles of Canada, boys! First Battalion!

> *DEIGHTON reads the company banner.*

Volens et Valens! Whatever that means.

RECRUITER: Willing and able, boys. Willing and able.

RALPH: I like the sound of that.

DEIGHTON: I can't wait to shoot me some Krauts.

COOPER: Right between their beady eyes. KA-POW! KA-POW!

(a realization) Hey. We're men now, boys. We need to get liquored up and get ourselves some girls! C'mon!

DEIGHTON and COOPER run off firing their imaginary guns. RALPH looks at the banner for a beat.

RALPH: *Volens et Valens . . .*

RALPH turns to address the audience. MITSUE joins him.

To say we were young and naive . . .

MITSUE: The whole world was.

RALPH: Me and the boys thought we'd see a big chunk of it. England. France. Germany. But Canada wasn't even in the war. We spent our first nine months in the army guarding the airport in Gander. Lotta action. Lotta action . . .

He exits.

MITSUE: For Miyoko and me, our biggest worry was . . . boys. And what to do after high school. Because . . . boys. Girls were expected to get married. A high school education was more than enough for a girl. Maybe even too much . . .

MIYOKO enters and plunks down by their tree.

MIYOKO: *Mo! [Uggh!]* I can't go to the movies Sunday, Mits. I have to get pictures taken. For the *nakodo*. The matchmaker.

MITSUE: No. Already?

MIYOKO: You would not believe how much money my parents are paying this guy—my jaw almost hit the floor when I found out. We couldn't afford nursing school after this even if I got in. *Your* family's rich at least—your dad has two boats *and* the cod licence for winter.

MITSUE: I don't know if that makes him rich. I think it just means he has to work twice as hard.

MIYOKO: Well everyone thinks he's *o-kane-mochi [very rich]*. Which makes you the biggest catch in Celtic.

MITSUE: *Yamete, mo! [Stop it!]* That's it. Once we graduate, we're running off to the West End together.

MIYOKO: Oh I lie in bed and dream about it.

MITSUE: Don't think *I* don't. Can you just see us, in a cute little apartment on English Bay? With actual plaster walls and ceilings?

MIYOKO: Why can't it be? Sometimes I could just cry.

MITSUE: I know, *ne?*

MITSUE's older brother PAT enters, his hair immaculately pomaded.

MIYOKO: Hi, Pat!

PAT: Hey, Miyoko.

MIYOKO: Your hair looks nice.

PAT: Oh? It's nothing.

MIYOKO: Maybe see you Sunday? If you're going for a drive.

PAT: Yeah, maybe.

MITSUE: You just told me you're not free on Sunday.

MIYOKO: I don't have time to go to the movies. But I could go for a drive.

MITSUE: Miyoko!

PAT: I'll let you know.

(to MITSUE) You gotta come home now.

MITSUE: It's still early.

PAT: Dad wants to talk to you.

The girls get up.

MIYOKO: What did you do, Mits? Are you in trouble?

MITSUE: Am I? Who knows. I'll see you tomorrow, I guess.

MIYOKO: *Un. Ja-ne. [Okay. Later.]*

MIYOKO starts off.

PAT: Hey, I'll walk you home.

MIYOKO is pleased. As she and PAT head off:

MIYOKO: West End, Mits! West End!

MITSUE crosses to TOMI. YOSUKE enters, pensive.

MITSUE: Papa?

YOSUKE: Sit. Have to discuss something.

They sit.

MITSUE: What is it?

YOSUKE: Mmm.

YOSUKE looks to TOMI.

TOMI: Mitsue, Papa *ga ne*, he receive . . . a marriage proposal for you.

MITSUE: What! Who?

YOSUKE: Yanagisawa *no . . . chonan dakke? [Yanagisawa's . . . is it the eldest?]* Takahiro?

TOMI: *Chigau. Jinan no Takanori desho. [Wrong. It's the second son, Takanori.]*

YOSUKE: Takanori? *Sokai? [Is that right?]*

TOMI: *So desho, otosan, nani yutteno? [Of course that's right. What are you saying?]*

(to MITSUE) It's Takanori. You know him.

MITSUE: Of course I know him. We were born three days apart.

YOSUKE: Yeah, that kid. His father ask me. I say, they not finish high school till June. He say, wanna get head start. So. What you think?

MITSUE: Papa. Why would I want to marry him? I've known him my whole life and he's barely said ten words to me the whole time.

YOSUKE: My father only say three words to my mother. *(mimes)* *Meshi , furo, futon!* [*Food, bath, bed!*] Not unusual for Japanese guy.

TOMI: *Fuzakenaide*, Papa. [*Stop joking.*] We have to take serious for Mitsue. This is serious for her.

YOSUKE: Mm. *Ma.* [*Well.*] This is only first one. More coming. What you wanna do?

MITSUE: Well . . . after high school . . . I'd like to keep studying. To be a teacher.

YOSUKE: That's good dream, Mitsue. Me and Mama not against, okay? Some Japanese woman have done before. But . . . no one will hire.

TOMI: We know one woman from Powell Street, she go to Alberta to teach. *Inaka [the country]* where there's no teacher. She come back to BC, many years experience, but can't find work. She have private class now teaching English to *issei*.

YOSUKE: Basically she is just a English tutor, *ne*. And students have no money, so . . .

MITSUE: Times are changing, Papa.

YOSUKE: Yes. But maybe not fast enough for you. Meantime, you have to work, earn money, maybe start family. So. Try think something you can do right away.

MITSUE: Right away?

TOMI: Papa not saying give up your dream, Mitsue. But BC is *hakujin shakai.* White society, *desho? [Right?]* So you need backup plan.

YOSUKE: *Nipponjin* always need backup plan. And insurance. Always need backup and insurance. Think about this, okay?

He gets up.

By the way, if you see Yanagisawa, or any other guy propose to you, have to be careful how you say no, okay? Our family, their family— it's business.

He exits.

TOMI: *Ocha nomou ka? [Want some tea?]*

MITSUE, crestfallen, shakes her head.

Mitsue. *Kuyashii kamo shirenaikedo . . . [I know you're disappointed but . . .]* Tell Papa thank you, okay? Everything he do, he always working hard for us, *ne?* We are lucky. So lucky . . .

Lights up on RALPH in his bedroom in Calgary. We hear a woman's voice calling from off stage:

PHYLLIS: *(off stage)* Ralph? It's time for work . . .

RALPH agitatedly paces, squeezing his eyes shut, holding his head in his hands. Whenever he looks up, a JAPANESE SOLDIER is there in the shadows. PHYLLIS knocks at the door.

PHYLLIS: Ralph?

RALPH wills himself together, picks up a Bible, and pretends to peruse.

RALPH: Yeah.

PHYLLIS enters. The JAPANESE SOLDIER recedes into darkness.

PHYLLIS: Are you going to work today?

RALPH: Of course I'm going to work.

PHYLLIS: You'll be late.

RALPH: I got a couple minutes for a daily Psalm.

PHYLLIS: That's the Book of Mark. Same page you always read.

RALPH: You know what I mean.

PHYLLIS: Sweetheart? Is it bad today?

RALPH: I'm fine.

PHYLLIS: Ralph MacLean. I know that look in your eye.

He stares at her with exaggerated googly eyes.

RALPH: *I'm fine.*

She doesn't buy it but moves on.

PHYLLIS: Diane called.

RALPH: Yeah.

PHYLLIS: That Japanese boy she's seeing. Stanley. His mother is worried about what to cook for you.

RALPH: That's happening, is it?

PHYLLIS: She's taken a shine to him. But we don't have to go.

RALPH: I'm game for anything. You're the one they should worry about. You'll look at a plate of wontons like the Chinese who made it moved in next door.

PHYLLIS: That is not true.

RALPH: You're a little suspicious, Phyllis, when it comes to anything unfamiliar. Especially food.

PHYLLIS: I've tried many unfamiliar foods. I just don't like soy sauce. It's too salty for me.

RALPH: Salt is too salty for you. Ever since you found out too much salt is bad for people with high blood pressure, you think it's bad for anybody in any amount. Men were dying in the camps because they didn't have it. Good men. Salt of the earth.

A beat. He starts putting on a shirt.

Time to go.

PHYLLIS: Why don't you call in. Stay home.

RALPH: I'm better off working. Any man is.

PHYLLIS: You know, I could bring a meatloaf or a casserole so she doesn't have to worry.

RALPH: Phyllis. You are judging this woman's cooking before you have had so much as a taste. Is that Christian? Is that even neighbourly?

PHYLLIS: So we're going then?

RALPH: Like I said, I'm game.

He leaves. PHYLLIS *picks up a phone on a night table and dials.*

PHYLLIS: Hi, sweetheart, it's Mum. Mm-hm. Just ask her to go light on the soy sauce. Mm-hm. Oh, and . . . *(sotto)* Maybe mention the peaches. Okey-dokey. Well we'll see you soon, sweetheart. Can't wait. Love you. Mean it!

SCENE 8

YOSUKE, TOMI, and PAT sit in the front room of their house, listening to war news on the radio.

CBC RADIO: (*voice-over*) The CBC news for May 14, 1940. Newly appointed British prime minister Winston Churchill addressed his House of Commons today as the Nazi invasion of Europe struck deeper into Belgium and France.

CHURCHILL: (*voice-over*) "I have nothing to offer but blood, toil, tears, and sweat. We have before us an ordeal of the most grievous kind. We have before us many, many long months of struggle and of suffering . . . "

MITSUE bursts in with her book bag, late for school.

MITSUE: The war again? What's happening over there?

YOSUKE: Sit. Family meeting.

MITSUE: I'll be late. And I have to see if Miyoko is okay. Finals are coming up and she hasn't been at school all week.

TOMI: Mitsue. We have something to talk to you. Miyoko have to take test. It's . . . *Kekkaku na no. Wakaru?* [*It's tuberculosis. Understand?*] So. You have to take test also.

MITSUE: *Kekkaku?*

PAT: It's TB, Mits. Tuberculosis.

MITSUE: That can't be . . . She wasn't coughing or anything. She wasn't sick at all.

TOMI: It doesn't always go in lungs. Sometimes bones, other places.

YOSUKE: If you are sick, we all have to take.

PAT: I'm sure we'll be fine, Dad—we have a healthy lifestyle. Some of the families around here, though—they're too Japanese.

MITSUE: Too Japanese? You're going out with her—

TOMI: What?

MITSUE: You take her for a drive every Sunday—

YOSUKE: What mean "too Japanese"?

PAT: I'm not going out with her. I just drive her around now and then.

YOSUKE: Pat. What mean "too Japanese"? Japanese is Japanese. You are Japanese. We are Japanese.

PAT: You know what I mean. You and Mom make an effort. You try to speak English; you're open to Canadian food. Milk, bread, and beef sometimes instead of tea, rice, and fish. We bathe in our own *ofuro*, we don't go in the *sento* with everybody. Some of the old ways are backward and unhealthy.

MITSUE: You're horrible!

PAT: I'm just calling it like I see it. The paper says Japanese and Chinese have four times the rate of TB that whites have. Four times—

MITSUE: Dirty knees, is that it? We get TB because of our dirty knees?

She gets up.

TOMI: Where you going?

MITSUE: I'm going to see her. I have to!

TOMI: Mitsue! You can't! *Da-me! [Don't!]*

MITSUE runs from the house to the oak tree in the park.

MITSUE: Please be okay, Miyoko, please please be okay . . . Please God, Heavenly Father, *kami-sama*, whoever's up there . . . please please please let her be okay . . . One-two-three-four-five I'm alive! One-two-three-four-five . . .

Animation: MITSUE and MIYOKO are playing patty-cake under the tree. MIYOKO floats away into the sky. MITSUE stands and watches her friend go. We see MITSUE grow from a teen into a young woman.

On stage, MITSUE crosses into MRS. YAMAMOTO's dress shop.

Title: Granville Street, Vancouver. Summer 1941.

MRS. YAMAMOTO: (*occasionally speaking Japanese in a Hiroshima dialect*) *Nihongo de ehh kana?* [*Is Japanese all right?*]

MITSUE: *Ah, hai, mochiron.* [*Ah, yes, of course.*]

MRS. YAMAMOTO: *Demo eigo de ikouka. Okyakusama eigo da shi.* [*But let's go with English. The customers speak English.*] I'm so happy you are fluent, Mitsue-chan. My customer mostly very proper lady from Shaughnessy. I want them be comfortable.

MITSUE: Thank you for this opportunity, Yamamoto-san. I promise you I'm a hard worker.

MRS. YAMAMOTO: Of course! *Nihon-jin jyaro!* [*You're Japanese!*] And being Japanese I know you can sew a kimono. What's most important is you are comfortable with latest Western fashion and technique.

MITSUE: French seams, princess seams, invisible zippers—I learned it all in school, Mrs. Yamamoto.

MRS. YAMAMOTO: I know. I check with your teacher.

MITSUE: Oh?

A beat.

Do . . . um . . . many men from the neighbourhood come in as well?

MRS. YAMAMOTO: Men? Why?

MITSUE: Oh, I just . . . I have a lot of experience mending things and doing alterations for my father and my brother Pat and . . . and so on.

MRS. YAMAMOTO: Sometime ladies bring husband's *wai-shatsu* and *zubon*. But we are dress shop. Gentleman tailor across the street. Mr. Archibald.

(joking) You want work there instead?

MITSUE: Oh no! *Sumimasen.* How silly of me.

MRS. YAMAMOTO: So, when can you start, Mitsue-chan? Tomorrow okay?

MITSUE: Tomorrow? I can start now if you like.

MRS. YAMAMOTO: I was hoping you say that. Come.

She picks up a dress in progress and leads MITSUE off. They exit. Elsewhere, RALPH says goodbye to his MOTHER. He's wearing the warm-weather uniform he's been issued: short-sleeved khaki shirt and shorts.

RALPH: I won't be home again for a while. We're shipping out as soon as we get back from this furlough.

MOTHER: You sure you joined the army? You're dressed for a Boy Scout jamboree.

RALPH: Close. *(sotto)* Rumour has it, Jamaica. POW camp there with Nazi prisoners.

MOTHER: I'm happy as long as you stay out of harm's way. And you come home in one piece, you hear.

She hands him his army-issued rucksack.

RALPH: I will.

He looks inside the pack.

Peaches! Three cans? That's too much. The army feeds me good. You keep these and treat the little ones.

MOTHER: Take one at least. I know you love 'em.

RALPH: Thank you, Mother.

He gives his mother a hug and a peck on the cheek. As he turns to go:

MOTHER: Ralph. Say goodbye to your father.

Lights up on RALPH's FATHER lying in bed, his breathing a death rattle. RALPH watches him for a long beat.

RALPH: Goodbye, Father. Good riddance.

He turns to the audience. MITSUE joins him.

Jamaica. I won't name names, but even when we got on a train headed west some of the boys still thought we were going there. After a year doing nothing more dangerous than chasing off flocks of seagulls, the idea that we were headed off to war looking like this—it never once crossed our minds.

MITSUE: The idea that I couldn't be a teacher, that Miyoko could never have been a nurse, that dressmaking was just about the only job open to Japanese women aside from being a maid or working in a cannery—it was a rude awakening. Don't get me wrong—I loved working for Mrs. Yamamoto. And I had so much hope and faith that better days were just around the corner . . .

RALPH exits. MITSUE crosses back to the dress shop and . . .

A rather glamorous and self-absorbed young white woman
enters.

YOUNG WOMAN: (*examining the alterations on her dress*) This will do
nicely. I don't mind telling you—you do very good work. Well done.

MITSUE: Thank you.

YOUNG WOMAN: I have so many end-of-summer engagements the
next few weeks. Perhaps I'll call on you again.

MITSUE: Please do. It would be our pleasure. Enjoy your evening.

YOUNG WOMAN: Oh, I shall.

The YOUNG WOMAN leaves. MITSUE turns to MRS. YAMAMOTO,
who is tidying up in the back.

MITSUE: Yamamoto-san? Will that be all for today?

MRS. YAMAMOTO: *Hai domo, gokuro-sama. [Yes, thank you for your*
help.] My customer so happy with you, Mitsue-chan. "Oh, your new
girl such good worker! And her English so good!"

MITSUE: That's . . . nice to know. Thank you for telling me,
Yamamoto-san.

As MITSUE gets ready to go, MRS. YAMAMOTO pretends to
remember something.

MRS. YAMAMOTO: Oh, Mitsue-chan . . .

MITSUE: Yes?

MRS. YAMAMOTO: *Sakamoto-san no musuko-san ga ne . . . Hanashita desho? [Mrs. Sakamoto's son . . . I mentioned him.]* He is coming next week. He want to meet you. Okay?

MITSUE: Um . . . okay. Why does he want to meet me?

MRS. YAMAMOTO: He saw you.

MITSUE: He did?

MRS. YAMAMOTO: Yes, through window. Last week, and two weeks before. And two weeks before. He come in Vancouver every two weeks. And look through window. Now he want to meet you. Okay?

(off MITSUE's look) Sonna—shinpainai! Atama mo iishi, totemo johin na kata desu. Hai. [Oh please—don't worry! He's smart and he's a very refined person. Yes.] I'm thinking for you, Mitsue-chan.

MITSUE: Yamamoto-san, that's . . . so thoughtful of you. *Arigato-gozaimasu.*

> *They bow. MITSUE boards the bus home to Celtic. She stands, packed in among the other passengers. All the other passengers are white, several of whom are either glaring or casting sideways glances her way. MITSUE stares out the window.*

Oh, Miyoko. It's times like this I miss you most. I feel so at home working for Mrs. Yamamoto, but then I get on this bus and all the little sideways glances and dirty looks make me feel like I don't belong. How dare I be on this bus, in their presence, in their line of vision, in their city, their province, their country. If only you were here I wouldn't mind so. If you were here I bet we wouldn't even be going home right now, Miyoko. We'd have gone straight to the Stanley to see a movie. And we'd sit wherever we pleased, too! You'd just love the movie playing right now—*How Green Was My Valley.* It's about a coal mining town in Wales, but it could just as easily be about us Japanese. The Welsh are so like us. They work and toil for nothing, nothing but pride and family. There's a dreamy new actor in it, Miyoko—Roddy McDowall.

MITSUE swoons.

Oh, and you know who came into the dress shop today? A new woman, not much older than me. She looked just like Maureen O'Hara—she was Esmeralda in *The Hunchback of Notre Dame*, remember? And she's in *How Green Was My Valley* also. Anyway, I so wished you were there because I wanted to whisper to Mrs. Yamamoto, "She looks just like Maureen O'Hara," but I knew Mrs. Yamamoto would have no idea what I was talking about . . .

MITSUE is suddenly overcome with sadness.

And neither would you, Miyoko. You never saw *The Hunchback of Notre Dame*.

She looks out the window.

Oh no. It's Joji Ishida. And he has flowers! Uggggh! God help me, Miyoko.

The bus stops. MITSUE gets off and looks up to the sky.

Talk to you tomorrow . . .

MITSUE turns to face her suitor, JOJI, who has been waiting for her at the bus stop. He's made some effort to dress up, but he's not one to shine up like a new penny.

JOJI: Fancy meeting you here, Mitsue.

MITSUE: Hello, Joji.

JOJI: Going this way?

MITSUE: It's the way home.

JOJI: So it is. *(re: flowers)* These are for you. My mom grew them in her garden.

MITSUE: Thank you. They're lovely.

JOJI: So, listen, me and her have been talking, and honestly you'd be a big help to her. There's Dad and five of us boys she's gotta cook for, do laundry—

MITSUE: Joji, are you asking me to marry *you* or your mother? You don't love me. You just want a servant girl to help with the housework.

JOJI: Aw geez, there you go getting all sticky and modern talking about love and female emancipation. I'm as Canadian as you, Mits, but first we're Japanese. On second thought, what I should say is, *you're* as Japanese as *I am*. Being Canadian comes second.

She turns away.

Oh no you don't, now wait just a second! You can't turn your back on who you are. We're Japanese and marriage is more important than your hurt feelings!

She turns back to find JOJI transformed into her next suitor, MOTOHARU. He's considerably smoother.

MITSUE: I . . . I'm flattered, Motoharu. I didn't know you thought of me in that way.

MOTOHARU: Well it just makes sense. And I feel for you, Mits. I've heard through the rumour mill about these other Celtic boys, sending their fathers to talk to your father, falling back on traditional ways. I have to say I find it cowardly. And insulting to you. It's your choice, after all. I'm here because that doesn't scare me. I know you'll choose me.

MITSUE: I . . . I don't know if I have the same feelings for you . . .

MOTOHARU: Don't worry about that right now. You will. You're the most beautiful girl in Celtic, and not to sound cocky, but I'm the handsomest bachelor. All the women say so. It's only right that we should be together.

He falls to one knee.

Take my hand in marriage, Mitsue, and I will make you the happiest woman in the world. I know all about making you happy.

He takes her hand and kisses it.

MITSUE: What are you doing?

MOTOHARU: Darling. Don't be shy.

He stands, puts his hand on the small of her back, and pulls her close. He blows on the back of her neck. She slaps him.

MITSUE: What do you think you're doing? I'm telling your mother!

She wheels away.

MOTOHARU: My . . . No no no no, not my mother, Mits! I got carried away is all. Please. Not my mother!

She turns back to find MOTOHARU *transformed into* ICHIRO, *a young man who actually seems worthy of her.* MITSUE *turns to face him. For the first time we see that she is struggling with her decision.*

MITSUE: Ichiro . . .

ICHIRO: I'm going to UBC. I'm going to build myself a Canadian life and I'm never looking back. I would be honoured if you would walk by my side.

MITSUE: I'm honoured that you would ask me. It's just . . .

ICHIRO: I understand. *Love.* I think love grows from lesser feelings. I think you're beautiful. I admire you. Seeing you and being around you makes me happy. That scares me. I don't know if that's love, but I'm going to plant the seed, Mits, and I just know it's gonna grow into something strong and beautiful. And one day you'll see it, too. So I'm going to ask you every day until you say yes.

MITSUE: Please don't. I need time, Ichiro. Am I even ready for this?

ICHIRO: Close your eyes.

MITSUE: What?

ICHIRO: I'm not gonna do anything funny, Mits. Just close your eyes for me. Okay. Now picture a house, like the ones you see on your bus ride home. The ones you dream of living in. A nice yard, a dog, kids skipping rope and playing hockey in the driveway. Can you see yourself living there? Can you see us? I can. I know I got a shot, Mits. With you by my side, I know I can do it. A Canadian life. With kids who grow up Canadian. Who will never have to feel they don't belong. Tell me you can see it.

MITSUE: It's like a dream. Something I won't even dare to think about having.

ICHIRO: Mits. Let's make it happen. You and me. If we don't even try, what are we even doing?

She opens her eyes. Sees him in a new light.

SCENE 12

STAN and RALPH are on the porch of RALPH's house as in Scene 1.

STAN: I'm just . . . living my life, sir. Like any kid my age.

RALPH: You were to have Diane home by eleven.

STAN: We were here by ten forty-five, sir.

RALPH: She wasn't inside.

STAN: We were just talking out here on the lawn.

Beat.

I got her a helmet.

RALPH: You got her wearing bell-bottoms, too, don'tcha? And listening to rock and roll.

STAN: Look, Mr. MacLean . . . I know this is about more than my motorcycle and my clothes and having Diane home by eleven. I know you fought against men who looked like me, sir. I know you suffered a great deal at their hands—

RALPH: Are you out of your mind? Men who looked like you? You'd a lasted half a day.

STAN: All I ask is that you see me for who I am and treat me with fairness.

RALPH: You want to talk about fairness? I went off to war because it was the right thing to do.

STAN: Yes, sir.

RALPH: Nothing about it was fair. Not a damn thing.

STAN: Yes, sir.

RALPH: Fairness! Let's talk about respect. My daughter, my house, my rules.

STAN: Sir, I've been nothing but respectful to you and Diane.

RALPH: Make sure you keep it that way. And if you have any intentions beyond this . . . summer dating or whatever it is, you come to me. Man to man.

STAN: Yes, sir. I hope we're still on for dinner at my parents' place in the Hat.

RALPH: That is entirely, *entirely* up to you. Do you understand?

STAN: Yes, sir.

> STAN *crosses to* MITSUE *in her kitchen.*

MITSUE: Easy on the soy sauce. And no canned peaches.

STAN: Yeah, she said she seems to remember a time when he was served it at a picnic or something and he got real quiet and went off into the woods, and he didn't come back for a long time. It started getting dark and they had to go looking for him.

MITSUE: My goodness. Poor man. And they're sure it was the canned peaches? Fresh peaches, okay?

STAN: I dunno. Do you even have any? Were you going to serve them?

MITSUE: Well what about fruit salad? Or fruit cocktail?

STAN: We don't have to prepare for every hypothetical, Mother.

MITSUE: God forbid I ruin everything because I served fruit cocktail. You'd never forgive me.

STAN: What *is* the menu, if I may ask?

MITSUE: Well I thought we'd have *osenbei [rice crackers]* and almond *choco* for appetizers—everybody likes those. My famous chow mein—easy on the soy sauce—sweet-and-sour spareribs, barbecued BC sockeye. And *gohan [steamed rice]*.

STAN: So not really Japanese then.

MITSUE: *I'm* making it, Stanley, so it is Japanese. It's Canadian Japanese. Anyway, you were worried if he could eat *nihon-ryori [Japanese food]* so I steered away.

STAN: Uh-huh.

MITSUE: You don't seem to approve. I can heat up some Chef Boyardee if that's all you're interested in.

STAN: It just occurs to me that he served in China and was put in a camp there *before* he got sent to Japan, so . . . You know what, maybe I better check if he's okay with Chinese food just to be safe.

MITSUE: You really like this girl, don't you?

STAN: Sure I like her. You know. I just want everybody to get along. You have a dessert planned?

MITSUE: Oh . . . I was thinking a peach upside-down cake, peach cobbler, Jello fruit cocktail . . . And fortune cookies. Your father came home from making deliveries with three big sacks! *Mo doshio-monai!* [*I'm done!*]

    They share a chuckle.

STAN: I want you and Dad to have a good time, too. I don't want there to be any reason for awkwardness.

    A beat.

What about Tomi *obaachan?*

MITSUE: She'll probably just stay in her room.

STAN: But what if . . . ? Aw heck—what am I even worrying about? Just work your magic, Mom. Whatever you do is gonna be great.

    He gives her a hug and starts off. He notices she's just standing there, overcome by some emotion.

You okay?

MITSUE: *Obaachan* . . . My mama. I wish you could have known the woman she was before the war. I wish you could have known all of us. Your dad and me, we were just about your age. And despite everything we were happy. So happy . . .

> *HIDEO enters, dressed snappily and carrying a book. It is circa 1941. MITSUE sees him, likes what she sees. She takes off her apron, composes herself, and joins him on a park bench.*

SCENE 14

HIDEO: (*passes her the book*) For you. Yamamoto-san say you enjoy reading.

MITSUE: Thank you, I do. *I'm a Stranger Here Myself* by Ogden Nash. What is it about?

HIDEO: What is it about. It's collection of funny poems, funny ideas. The title catch my attention. I'm trying to read couple books every week to improve my English.

MITSUE: But . . . Yamamoto-san said you're Canadian?

HIDEO: Yes, born in Canada. My father sent me back to Japan so I don't get too Westernized. Not fair, *ne*? Canada is my home. I came back as soon as I can, and I am reading books to catch up. I don't mind—I love to read. And Yamamoto-san say you want to be a teacher. So I take a chance you will appreciate a book.

MITSUE: Well that's very thoughtful of you.

HIDEO: Also, this will give us something to talk about. Very sneaky, *ne*?

He gets a chuckle out of her. He takes the book, flips through some pages, and shows her something.

MITSUE: (*reads*) "The door of a bigoted mind opens outwards so that the only result of the pressure of facts upon it is to close it more snugly." Oh, Hideo, that's not funny—that's so true.

HIDEO: That's so true. I think so. But most Canadians are good people. And their mind will open from the inside.

MITSUE: I believe that, too.

He motions to a cross necklace she is wearing.

HIDEO: May I ask . . . your cross. Very beautiful.

MITSUE: Oh, thank you. It's from my friend Miyoko. We taught Sunday school together at the Japanese church. She . . . passed away.

HIDEO: I'm so sorry.

MITSUE: A lot of Japanese families in Celtic go to church. It's mainly a social thing. Choir, bake sales. The way my parents explain it, in Japan everybody is Shinto and Buddhist . . . just in case. So now we're in Canada, we're all *Christian* and Buddhist *just in case.*

HIDEO laughs.

HIDEO: Good strategy.

MITSUE: Insurance and a backup plan. They're big on that, too.

HIDEO: Would you like to walk some more, Mitsue? May I call you Mitsue?

They walk.

MITSUE: Of course. My friends call me Mits. Shall I call you Hideo?

HIDEO: Of course. My friends call me . . . Bob.

MITSUE: *Bob?*

HIDEO: When I was young, *hakujin* can't say Hideo, so . . .

MITSUE: You don't look like a Bob. I'm gonna stick with Hideo.

HIDEO: I'm gonna stick with Mits.

MITSUE: Are you . . . repeating everything I say?

HIDEO: Oh. Yes. To improve my English.

MITSUE: All righty then.

HIDEO: All righty then!

> *They exit.* RALPH, DEIGHTON, *and* COOPER *enter opposite,
> entranced by the sights and sounds of Hong Kong.*

HONG KONG RADIO: A contingent of nearly two thousand Canadian troops arrived in Hong Kong this morning—reinforcements for the British garrison defending the colony . . .

DEIGHTON: Can you believe this—we're gonna live like kings! I was talking to one of the Tommies and he said you can hire a coolie to shine your shoes, wash your clothes, and shave you every morning—all for a quarter!

RALPH: Do you even need to shave, Deighton?

DEIGHTON: Sure I shave.

COOPER: Any Chinaman you hire is gonna shave the only hair he sees on your face—your eyebrows!

They laugh. A young Chinese woman walks by in a cheongsam.

God almighty. You can have her all day and night for a couple bucks, I bet.

DEIGHTON: Well that's no bargain. A coolie will do your housework for twenty-five cents.

COOPER: Whattaya—in kindergarten?

DEIGHTON: What?

COOPER: She's a Pick Me Up, bonehead. A pro skirt.

DEIGHTON: A what?

RALPH: She's a prostitute, Deighton.

DEIGHTON: Really? How can you tell?

COOPER: They all are. For a price.

DEIGHTON: Juuu-daaas. We're a long way from home now, ain't we, Ralphie?

RALPH: I'll say.

COOPER: Get a load of this—I heard half the officers live off-base with their concubines. One of the chaplains got himself a love nest, too.

DEIGHTON: Is that even allowed?

COOPER: Allowed?

DEIGHTON: We're supposed to comport ourselves a certain way. Aren't we? We're in the army.

COOPER: All's fair in love and war, boys. Hey, what say we follow Lotus Blossom there. She's bound to lead us somewhere interesting.

DEIGHTON: (*nervous*) Ohhh boy. Well, you know me, I'm up for anything. What say you, Ralphie?

RALPH: I'm gonna look for a souvenir for my ma.

COOPER: Well aren't you a wet shirt.

DEIGHTON: (*grateful for the out*) Well I can't leave Ralph all by his lonesome, Coop. He's bound to get all morose on us.

COOPER: I get it. You need to grow some hair on your figs before you partake. See ya boys later.

DEIGHTON: Shut up, Coop! I got hair! I *got* hair!

As they exit HIDEO and MITSUE enter again, on another date, holding hands now.

HIDEO: *Tsumari, Baberu-no-tou to tabunka kyosei wa mattaku kankeinai.*

MITSUE: I want you to tell me the exact same thing now in English.

HIDEO: *Mitsue-sensei kibishii! [You're so strict, Mitsue-sensei!]*

MITSUE: You want to keep improving, don't you? Isn't that the only reason you're dating me?

HIDEO: Oh, how did you guess?

　　MITSUE hits him playfully.

MITSUE: Humph. Go.

HIDEO: Okay. *Baberu-no-to.* Tower of Babel. *Tabunka kyosei.* Many culture together—

MITSUE: Multi.

HIDEO: Multi-culture together.

MITSUE: Ism. Multi-cultural-ism.

HIDEO: Multi-culture-together-ism. Yes. And Tower of Babel story. They are different things entirely.

MITSUE: Good.

HIDEO: A-plus?

MITSUE: C-plus.

HIDEO: What? I thought *nisei* girl supposed to be easy. You are too hard for me. I need *issei* girl.

MITSUE: Be my guest.

She sits on their bench. He joins her.

What *do* you see in me, I wonder? I mean, if I'm too much to handle.

HIDEO: Ohhh I like it, Mitsue Oseki. Smart. Modern. Individual. Canadian. A Canadian woman for a Canadian life. A Canadian family.

MITSUE: Is that . . . what you see for yourself?

HIDEO: I'm good with numbers, Mits. I will improve my English. I can get a good job. My wife . . . my wife will be an educated, independent woman.

MITSUE: Oh? Who is she? Have you met her yet?

HIDEO: Maybe.

MITSUE: Just maybe?

The moment is more intimate than they're ready for. MITSUE *looks away and discreetly pats her nose.*

HIDEO: Mits? Are you okay?

MITSUE: Oh, it's nothing, it's so silly. I was imaging myself sitting here, a modern, sophisticated woman, but then I realized, Mitsue Oseki, you're hardly wearing makeup, your nose must be so shiny!

HIDEO: No. Is my nose shiny?

She laughs. He watches her laughing.

Sugao ga ichiban. [*Natural beauty is best.*] What is *sugao* in English? Natural face? No makeup face?

MITSUE: Um . . . natural beauty?

HIDEO: Mits. You are natural beauty. But I prefer *sugao*. Because the *kanji* mean "honest face," *ne*? You are natural beauty with an honest face.

She leans in for the movie kiss of her dreams. He sits there like a puppy dog.

MITSUE: Kiss me, Hideo.

HIDEO: Here?

MITSUE: It's a free country.

He leans in awkwardly and gives her a little peck.

Bob Sakamoto. Have you ever been to the movies?

HIDEO: Yes?

MITSUE: I want you to kiss me like I've seen girls get kissed.

She looks at him with come-hither eyes, offering her lips to his. They kiss like they mean it.

That woman you're looking for. Now have you met her?

As they lose themselves in full make-out mode . . .

We hear faint booms in the distance. They get louder—they're explosions. We hear air-raid sirens, machine-gun fire at close range, and dive bombers screaming down from the sky.

Title: December 7, 1941.

HONOLULU RADIO: (*voice-over*) This is KTU in Honolulu, Hawaii ... We have witnessed this morning the severe bombing of Pearl Harbor by enemy planes, undoubtedly Japanese ... It is no joke. It is a real war ...

HONG KONG RADIO: (*voice-over*) This is Hong Kong, this is Hong Kong. We are at war with Japan. Kowloon has been bombed, some parts are burning ...

Pedestrians rush onto the stage.

PEDESTRIAN MAN 1: The Japs have attacked! It's on the radio. This is it. This is war!

MITSUE: What ... what did he say?

HIDEO: Japan is attacked?

PEDESTRIAN WOMAN: Oh my Lord, there's two right there!

PEDESTRIAN MAN 2: You Japs or Chinks?

HIDEO: No. We're not.

MITSUE: We're Canadian.

PEDESTRIAN MAN 1: They're Japs all right. Now get off the street before we kick you off.

HIDEO leads MITSUE away.

HIDEO: Mits. Not safe here. You have to go home. I will take you.

They run.

SCENE 17

Animation: A map of the Pacific Rim, smoke rising from the areas attacked by the Japanese. A montage of front-page headlines spins into view: "IT'S WAR!" "JAPS BOMB HAWAII—1500 DEAD." "JAPAN PLUNGES ASIA INTO WAR!" "JAPS ATTACK HAWAII, PHILIPPINES, GUAM, SINGAPORE." "HONG KONG HIT HARD—CANADIAN CASUALTIES MOUNT." "HONG KONG GARRISON UNDER SIEGE." A radio fades up:

CBC RADIO: (*voice-over*) . . . is now official. Canada is at war. The government of Prime Minister Mackenzie King announced moments ago that Canada has declared war on Japan . . .

MITSUE's mother, TOMI, and brother, PAT, are in the living room listening to the broadcast.

PAT: This has nothing to do with us.

TOMI: But we are Japanese. Living in Canada.

PAT: We're Canadian, Mom, so Canada's not at war with us. The Japs are.

TOMI: Pat—

PAT: It's their fault. The Japs!

TOMI: *Yamenasai! [Stop it!]*

PAT: You stop it. This is no time to be speaking Jap.

TOMI: There is no such language.

PAT: Good. Don't do it then.

TOMI: Eichi—

PAT: Don't call me that—

TOMI: Your name is Eichi. Children call you "Fatso," do you remember? Who make them change to "Pat"? I did. Don't forget. And don't talk to me about "Jap" in my house.

Voices are heard from off. MITSUE *and* HIDEO *enter.*

MITSUE: Mama? Mama!

TOMI: Oh Mitsue! Hideo-san! *Daijobu? Mo . . . taihen, taihen . . . [Are you okay? This is awful, so awful . . .]*

MITSUE *and* TOMI *embrace.* HIDEO *exchanges a nod with* PAT, *a quick bow with* TOMI.

MITSUE: Is everybody okay? Where's Dad?

PAT: He went down to the docks. See if anybody knows anything. What did you guys see out there?

MITSUE: People are angry . . . upset . . .

PAT: What do you expect? A sneak attack? Just like the Japs to pull a dirty trick like that.

TOMI: Eichi!

MITSUE: Pat—

PAT: Jap-Jap-Jap-Jap-Jap! What's it to you, Mits? That's what they are!

MITSUE: People call us that, too.

PAT: Because they don't see the difference. And if you go around acting like a Jap, that's your own fault. As for the rest of us, this is a chance to prove we're loyal Canadians. I'm enlisting first thing tomorrow morning.

TOMI: *Da-me.* *[No.]* You will not.

PAT: Why shouldn't I?

TOMI: You will not!

PAT: It's my duty as a Canadian. Whattaya say, Hideo? They'll need men like us. And I welcome the opportunity to prove my loyalty to Canada. We've been second-class citizens too long.

MITSUE: They won't take you, Pat. They won't let you enlist. They won't even let us vote—

PAT: They will after this. They have to.

YOSUKE enters. His expression is so grave that no one says a word.

TOMI: *Otosan . . . Do shimashita? [What happened?]*

YOSUKE shakes his head. After a beat he addresses everyone in English.

YOSUKE: They are taking our boats. Police have closed the docks. We cannot go near.

PAT: What did you say to them, Dad? You *issei* don't know how to talk to white people. I'm going down there to straighten things out.

YOSUKE: Pat. Don't make trouble. They are making arrest already—

PAT: Don't make trouble? They're not arresting me. I'm Canadian. We're the good guys and they need to see that! I'll enlist on the spot if I have to, but they have to understand I'm not a Jap! They have to!

PAT storms off. YOSUKE slumps into a chair. The others gather around him . . .

Animation: The idyllic images of Celtic Cannery now tainted by war. The police impound Japanese fishing boats on the Fraser River, a thousand of them tied together, as far as the eye can see. Japanese homes and businesses are boarded up and covered with graffiti: "JAPS OUT!" "LEAVE NOW OR DIE!" "THIS IS WAR!"

We hear gunfire, artillery, and roaring engines. A squadron of Japanese Zero fighters appear in the sky and now we are in Hong Kong. The Zeros dive down from the sky and strafe soldiers dug into a hillside, leaving death and destruction in their wake . . .

RALPH enters exhausted, covered in dirt and sweat, decked out for battle: Tommy helmet, ankle boots, knee-high socks, a pack and canteen, Bren gun, bandoliers of ammo over his "Boy Scout" warm-weather uniform.

RALPH: They hit us just three weeks after we arrived. There were 14,000 in the Hong Kong garrison: Brits, Indian sepoys, and us Canadians as green as the first leaves of spring. Our Jeeps and trucks had been rerouted to the Philippines. The British air support and artillery were down in Singapore. And there were 50,000 battle-hardened Japanese, wave after wave of them, coming across the harbour from the mainland. We were the first Canadian infantry soldiers in World War II. The first to fight, the first to die. The first to wonder what true patriot love means on a bloody hillside eight thousand miles from home . . .

Title: Canadian HQ, Palm Villa, Hong Kong. December 21, 1941.

An explosion brings us into the chaos of the makeshift Canadian HQ. RALPH staggers in and collapses as soon as he's in the door. COOPER sees him and scrambles over.

COOPER: Ralph! Ralphie! What a sight for sore eyes!

RALPH: Coop?

COOPER: You hurt?

RALPH: I just can't carry this shit anymore. I haven't slept in a week.

COOPER: Tell me about it.

RALPH: Any water?

COOPER hands RALPH a canteen and helps him ditch the equipment and ammunition.

Where's Deighton?

COOPER: I haven't seen him since the fighting started. It's bad, Ralph.

They're quiet, realizing DEIGHTON may very well be dead. The C.O., MORTIMER, comes over.

MORTIMER: MacLean? That you? Where you coming from, son?

RALPH: We were hauling ammo up Mount Parker, sir, but halfway there we met the survivors coming down. There's nothing left.

MORTIMER: Not much left here either. Catch your breath, then right back at it.

MORTIMER moves off to speak on the field telephone.

COOPER: We're done for, Ralph.

RALPH: Whattaya talking about. *Volens et valens*, right?

COOPER: We may be willing, but we sure ain't able. We got no trucks, no guns, no ammo, no planes, no nothing. We never had a fucking chance.

RALPH: C'mon, Coop. We're Grindstone boys. Put your nose to it.

MORTIMER strides to the centre of the room.

MORTIMER: All right, men, here's the skinny! Stanley Fort is taking heavy fire. If we lose it, it's all over. I need ten men. We're gonna dig in around the perimeter with our Bren guns and keep the Japs from setting up their heavy mortars.

RALPH: Sir, looks like you've only got the one Bren I brought to spare.

MORTIMER: We'll have to make do then. Gear up, let's get cracking.

RALPH gets to his feet.

COOPER: (*sotto*) Don't go.

RALPH: We're fish in a barrel sittin' here.

COOPER: Goddammit to hell, Ralph . . . I don't know what to do. I just want a real choice. A fighting chance!

RALPH: You know how to pray?

COOPER: Between you and me? You're the pastor.

RALPH: For real, Coop.

COOPER: Just make it up.

RALPH: Okay.

RALPH gets down next to COOPER.

Heavenly Father . . . me and Coop and the rest of us Canadian boys are about to go into battle. We are outnumbered, Lord, and our situation is desperate. We ask for strength, your mercy and protection. We are your sons, Lord, and we ask this in the name of *your* son, Jesus Christ. Amen.

COOPER: Not too shabby, MacLean. Amen.

RALPH: I'll see ya, Coop.

COOPER: I'm coming with you.

They grab their rifles and join MORTIMER.

MORTIMER: What are we working with?

COOPER: MacLean's Bren gun. The three bandoliers he brought with him. Five grenades. Three-oh-three shells for one, maybe two fights. Three cans of bully beef. Three cans of water.

MORTIMER: We'll take turns carrying the Bren.

RALPH: *(shouldering the machine gun)* I'll take first shift, sir.

MORTIMER: All right. Let's move out. Suppressing fire!

We hear the staccato of machine-gun fire.

Move! Move! Move!

MORTIMER, RALPH, and COOPER *run out and hit the deck.*

Animation: The silhouettes of seven other Canadian soldiers running with them. The treeline beyond swarms with enemy soldiers. Bullets buzz through the air. Muzzle flashes strobe from the dark woods. Grenades explode. We hear the distant roar of a plane engine.

RALPH: Plane! Plane! Take cover!

COOPER panics and runs out into the open.

COOPER: I'm going back!

MORTIMER: Cover! Get down!

MORTIMER runs out and tackles COOPER. The Zero bears down on them.

MacLean! Keep him off! Keep him off!

RALPH props the Bren gun on its tripod, kneels behind it, and starts firing.

Animation: The plane screams down on top of the soldiers, guns blazing. It banks off.

The Canadians regroup. COOPER is hyperventilating, terrified out of his mind. MORTIMER tries to calm him.

That was some firing, MacLean. I thought he had us dead to rights—

A grenade explodes. A hail of bullets. COOPER falls and screams, clutching his leg. The Canadians are again pinned down by unrelenting enemy fire.

Fall back! Every man for himself!

RALPH: Coop!

RALPH grabs COOPER, who is sitting in the middle of the fire-fight. RALPH scans for safety and sees a small mound of cover.

There, Coop! Over there!

COOPER: I can't! My leg!

RALPH drags COOPER behind the mound.

Jesus help me, I'm shot! I'm done for!

RALPH: Quiet, Coop! Shut up! Shut up!

RALPH tries to calm COOPER and keep them hidden from the enemy. There is a lull in the battle. RALPH takes a look at COOPER's leg. COOPER moans.

Shhh . . . Lemme see . . .

COOPER: Is it bad?

RALPH: We gotta surrender. We gotta get you to a hospital.

COOPER: No fucking way. Let's wait till they're gone. We'll sneak back to HQ.

RALPH: If they see us they'll shoot. They'll kill us. It's better we surrender.

COOPER: No, Ralph, please!

RALPH: You're bleeding bad, Coop. We gotta get your leg looked at. You wanna walk again, don'tcha?

COOPER: I'm scared of 'em, Ralph. I'm scared of 'em.

RALPH: Me, too. But we'll stick together. I won't let you outta my sight.

COOPER doesn't want to relent, but he gives RALPH a small nod. RALPH carefully gets up.

Hey! We surrender! Don't shoot! Don't shoot!

RALPH moves down stage and is joined by MITSUE.

I thought my war was over.

MITSUE: Me, too. After the first panic, I thought people would see we weren't going to hurt anybody. And they'd just leave us alone.

RALPH: I actually convinced myself that we *would* be going home. I mean, why would anybody want prisoners? You gotta lock 'em up, guard 'em, feed 'em, look after 'em. Just let me go home. It's not like I'm gonna come back here. Not ever.

MITSUE: Home felt safe. For a little while. Even when people started getting notices that they had to move away, I told myself it won't be for long. The war is on the other side of the ocean. I'm just a girl who wants to be a teacher. You went to school with me. We sang in the choir together. I hemmed your party dress.

RALPH returns to COOPER and helps him limp off.

RALPH: Hey! We're done! We give up! Help us, please . . .

MITSUE crosses to MRS. YAMAMOTO's dress shop to see a middle-aged man—MR. ARCHIBALD—and a couple of his helpers carrying boxes and bundles away.

MITSUE: Yamamoto-san . . . What's happening?

MRS. YAMAMOTO: Ah, Mitsue-chan. Mr. Archibald, tailor shop across street, he offer to keep my things.

MITSUE: Keep your things?

MRS. YAMAMOTO: I get the notice. Government say I have to go camp. Place called New Denver. I have sewing machines, expensive fabric. I cannot take with me and not safe here, so Mr. Archibald keep safe for me.

MITSUE: Yamamoto-san, I wish you had asked me. We could have helped store your things for you. Or put them in the church in Celtic—that's what a lot of families are doing.

MRS. YAMAMOTO: *Daijobu.* I'm only allowed what I can carry, so it must be for a short time, *ne?* And I am lucky. Some people have only one day to pack. I have one week! *Ara . . .* Hideo-san . . .

HIDEO has appeared on the street outside, troubled.

MITSUE: Yamamoto-san, excuse me.

MITSUE goes outside to him. Once MITSUE leaves, MRS. YAMAMOTO breaks down in tears. She exits.

Hideo . . . What are you doing here?

HIDEO: My father decide he is taking our family back to Japan.

MITSUE: Your family? Everyone? Hideo, are you saying goodbye?

HIDEO: I don't want to. I want to stay. But government is forcing unmarried *nikkei* men away. I may be forced back, too.

MITSUE: But . . . you're a Canadian citizen.

HIDEO: Citizen, Canadian-born, doesn't matter.

MITSUE: That . . . can't be true. They're just rumours.

HIDEO: I'm afraid not.

MITSUE: So . . . you're being sent away? Without me? Where?

Beat.

Hideo, answer me!

HIDEO: I didn't want to do it like this.

MITSUE: Do what? Hideo . . .

HIDEO: They are trying to separate us, Mits. But there is a chance we can stay together . . . if we are husband and wife.

He produces a ring box.

I was saving this for beautiful day in spring when *sakura* are blooming. I was going to write poem for you. But I have no poem, no beautiful words. Only my love and my promise.

He kneels.

Mitsue Oseki. I will devote my life to you. Will you marry me?

She embraces him.

MITSUE: This *is* a beautiful day. And your words are the most beautiful I could ever hope to hear. Our lives will be beautiful, Hideo. I just know it. We'll get through this. We'll get through this as long as we have each other . . .

Passersby gather ominously, glaring at HIDEO *and* MITSUE.

HIDEO: We better go.

Church bells ring. HIDEO *walks* MITSUE *to her home.* TOMI *enters and helps* MITSUE *into a simple homemade wedding dress.*

A wet winter day. A POLICE OFFICER *enters to guard the entrance to the church.* MITSUE'S *father,* YOSUKE, *enters with umbrellas for the ladies. He passes one to* TOMI, *who goes ahead. As* MITSUE *and* YOSUKE *approach the church,* YOSUKE *steps away from* MITSUE *to look at her.*

YOSUKE: If only they didn't take my camera.

MITSUE: Papa. Everyone's waiting.

Again, passersby gather, glaring with disapproval.

YOSUKE: They can wait. You are so beautiful. I want to remember these final moments you are my daughter, Oseki Mitsue.

MITSUE: I'll always be your daughter.

YOSUKE: A daughter is a child. But soon you will be Sakamoto Mitsue. A wife, and one day a mother.

POLICE OFFICER: Hey! Let's get this show on the road. I need your Jap registration cards.

MITSUE: (*stressed but not hostile*) Just a minute!

POLICE OFFICER: What did you say to me? I can shut this circus down right now!

YOSUKE: Sorry! Coming! Mitsue, your card.

As they fumble for their cards, MITSUE'S *suitor,* ICHIRO, *enters without an umbrella, utterly drenched.*

MITSUE: Ichiro . . .

ICHIRO: Mits. Don't go.

YOSUKE: Taniguchi? *Nanno tsumori da? [Taniguchi? What do you think you're doing?]*

ICHIRO: Please, Mits. I love you.

MITSUE: If you love me, you wouldn't be here. Don't do this to me.

POLICE OFFICER: Let's go, missy! Tick-tock!

MITSUE: Yes, sorry, we're coming!

MITSUE fumbles in her purse with growing panic.

Oh my God. I don't have mine. It's not in here. I . . . I must have left it . . .

ICHIRO: It's a sign, Mits. Don't go, don't do this—

YOSUKE: Taniguchi!

ICHIRO: Please, Mits—

MITSUE: Stop, Ichiro!

POLICE OFFICER: Come on already. I don't have all day to wait on you Japs!

YOSUKE takes MITSUE's purse and goes through it calmly. He finds her ID and hands it to her.

YOSUKE: Almost arrested on your own wedding day.

YOSUKE and MITSUE hurry up to the door with the registration cards, ICHIRO following close behind.

ICHIRO: I'll wait for you, Mits. I'll wait for you always . . .

POLICE OFFICER: This church needs to be empty and locked in one hour, understood?

YOSUKE: Yes, understood.

POLICE OFFICER: As for your banquet, you are not exempt from curfew regulations. You will vacate the restaurant by seven thirty at the latest and you are all to be in your homes by eight p.m. sharp. Is that clear?

YOSUKE: Yes. Thank you.

MITSUE: Ichiro . . . I can see you in your dream house. With happy kids playing in the yard. You're going to have a Canadian life. And I'm going to be so happy for you. Please be happy for me.

The "Wedding March" begins. YOSUKE and MITSUE go inside followed by the POLICE OFFICER. ICHIRO weeps in the rain. A single bell tolls.

The JAPANESE GUARD emerges from the church with RALPH, COOPER, and MORTIMER as at the beginning of the play. MITSUE, HIDEO, and other family members follow the soldiers out and stand at the top of the steps, the most funereal wedding party one can imagine.

JAPANESE GUARD: YOU! STAND UP! STAND STRAIGHT! ALL! STAND STRAIGHT!

RALPH does his best to get up. COOPER remains slumped, convulsing with pain.

COOPER: Ralph?

RALPH: I'm here, Coop. I'm right here.

The bell tolls. The JAPANESE GUARD looms over COOPER.

JAPANESE GUARD: You soldier? Why you cry like baby?

COOPER: My leg . . . My leg's shot . . .

MORTIMER: He needs a medic—a doctor. Doctor!

JAPANESE GUARD: Leg shot? I fix.

The GUARD kicks COOPER's leg. COOPER howls in pain. The bell tolls.

MORTIMER: Goddammit where is your commanding officer! I demand to speak to him!

JAPANESE GUARD: Soldier! Stop crying!

RALPH: Coop! Shhh! Take a breath—

JAPANESE GUARD: STOP CRYING!

The GUARD prods COOPER's leg again. COOPER howls louder. The bell tolls.

RALPH: Coop, no . . . NO . . . !

The GUARD suddenly draws his pistol and shoots COOPER in the head. Church bells suddenly peal in a cacophony, an expression not of joy but of madness.

HIDEO: Our lives will make up for this, Mits. I promise you. Our lives will make up for this.

End of Act I

Intermission: A montage of images from the internment: evac-uation notices, boarded-up Japanese businesses and homes, identity cards, long lines of families at Hastings Park and at train stations. These images are intercut with images of the Japanese occupation of Asia: triumphant Japanese troops, ruined cities, dead and terrified civilians, long lines of POWs marching to nowhere . . .

ACT II

PROLOGUE

RALPH and MITSUE sit on cots in their respective prisons. They make their way down stage and address the audience.

MITSUE: Hideo and I were married on January 29, 1942, less than two months after the attacks on Pearl Harbor and Hong Kong. We stayed at first with his parents in the boarding house they ran near Powell Street, until they went back to Japan for good. We weren't interned yet, but it already felt like a prison. Canada had betrayed Hideo's parents and they had grown to hate it. So when they looked at me, all they saw was a daughter-in-law who was too Canadian. *Too Canadian* . . .

RALPH: A thousand of us Royal Rifles went over to Hong Kong, a thousand more Winnipeg Grenadiers. In two weeks of fighting we suffered eight hundred Canadian casualties—nearly three hundred dead. We were kids, nineteen, twenty-year-old kids. Those of us still alive were thinking, "We survived this. This hell is over."

RALPH shakes his head.

By the end of February most of us were dying of sickness and malnutrition. Losing our hearing, our eyesight, our bowels, our minds. Losing even the will to sit up and lift ourselves out of our own filth. That was after just the first month. We were there nearly four more years.

MITSUE: For me, a girl too Canadian for my husband's parents but who could never be Canadian enough for the country I wanted to love . . . My war lasted seven more years. *Seven.* Or maybe seventy. Maybe it's going on still.

RALPH: This is the rest of our story. It's not easy, but . . . I'll tell you something. Knowing that somewhere out there in the world, love and kindness and humanity are waiting for you—your mother, your family, the friends you grew up with, an angel, a good Samaritan, somebody, somebody who cares—knowing they're out there gives you strength. So . . . come on. We'll get through this together.

> *MITSUE and RALPH light incense at a* butsudan, *a Japanese family altar. RALPH briefly pays his respects then exits. MITSUE prays.*

MITSUE's home in Medicine Hat. STAN enters the kitchen to find RON and TOMI eating contentedly in silence.

STAN: (*rummaging*) Anything left for me? Where's Mom?

RON: Downstairs. *Obaachan's butsudan.*

TOMI: *Osenko taiteru.* She pray. For Hiroshima.

STAN: Hiroshima's tomorrow, isn't it?

TOMI: *Nippon wa* already tomorrow.

STAN: Oh yeah. Why does Mom always take it so hard, I wonder. It's not like she had family or friends there. Did she, *obaachan*?

TOMI: Atomic bomb prove *hakujin* hate *nihonjin.* Prove!

TOMI abruptly gets up and exits. RON and STAN exchange shrugs. STAN has found some rice and okazu *and joins RON at the table.*

RON: So this dinner you're planning. I had a thought. Steak Diane. Ever heard of it?

STAN: No.

RON: It's steak cooked in butter in a very hot pan with chives and parsley. And then you pour sherry or brandy on it and . . . woosh! *It flames.* Huh? Is that Diane or what?

STAN: You wanna burn the house down? I like Mom's original menu. What do you care—you're not even gonna be here.

RON: Whoever you think we are, man, Japanese Canadians, Prairie boys, Albertans, whatever, I'm just saying, expand your mind. We can be a little more sophisticated than Mom's Japanese-slash-Chinese home cooking.

STAN: You mean more white.

RON: Whoa. It's just steak. With a little big-city flair.

STAN: It's not really who we are, Ron.

RON: We're whoever we want to be, that's what I'm saying. I'm a music promoter. A good one. You're gonna tell me that's not really who I am? Because why? Because I'm a hayseed from Medicine Hat? Or because I'm Japanese?

STAN: Well if we're free to be whoever we want to be I guess we're free to be Japanese, too. Japanese Canadian. Chow mein, spare ribs, barbecued salmon—

MITSUE enters.

MITSUE: What's wrong with my cooking?

She starts cleaning up after TOMI and RON.

STAN: Nothing, I was just telling Ron how much I like it.

RON: Open your mind, man. Right, Mom?

MITSUE: It would be fun to experiment. Steak Diane—

STAN: You told her?

MITSUE: And I was thinking iceberg-lettuce salad. And fondue.

STAN: Fondue.

MITSUE: It's a pot of melted cheese—

STAN: I know what fondue is.

MITSUE: It might be fun.

STAN: Can we have fun another time? After we make, you know, a normal first impression?

MITSUE: Stanley. If it's not going to be fun, why don't we call the whole thing off? Why are we getting all worked up trying to impress these people?

STAN: We're not getting worked up. Everything was fine until Elvis Beatle here got involved.

RON: Man, you are square. And I say this with love.

STAN: I'm square? Is my hair square? Are my jeans square? I ride a motorcycle, is that square? Why are you even part of this conversation? The original menu was fine, Mom. Please!

MITSUE: Have it your way then. I just thought the man's a war hero, I should cook up something special for him.

STAN: Your cooking *is* special. It's Japanese, it's Chinese, it's Canadian. I mean, you make those gyoza-perogy things. Where else you gonna get that?

RON: Steak Diane though. What Albertan is gonna turn down a Steak Diane?

STAN: Ron. The man fought in a war. You think it's a good idea to put a flaming hunk of meat in front of his face? Really?

STAN starts off.

And by the way, today's Hiroshima!

MITSUE: Light some *osenko.*

STAN: All right, I'm going.

STAN exits.

MITSUE: Ronnie, go light some *osenko* with your brother.

RON: Why exactly, Mom? "Just in case"? Me and Stan were wondering.

MITSUE: And he's down there doing it while you're up here asking a bunch of questions.

RON: You knew somebody there or what?

MITSUE: A lot of *issei* were from there. Everybody knew somebody.

RON: It did end the war though.

MITSUE: Not for me. Not for all of us Japanese from Celtic and Powell Street and Steveston and the islands up and down the coast. All the farmers out in the valley growing strawberries and tomatoes. The war ended but we weren't allowed back in BC, were we? Not for five more years. When they dropped the bomb, you know, I thought that *was* the end of it, and I was so happy because I thought I could go home. My heart was bursting I was so happy. So. Now I pray for Hiroshima. All those poor souls. I pray to ask their forgiveness.

Title: Shamshuipo POW *Camp, Hong Kong.* 1942.

RALPH and MORTIMER *stagger into the camp.*

MORTIMER: God almighty. There must be a thousand men in here.

Beat.

I'm gonna see who runs this joint. You try to find our Canadian boys.

MORTIMER exits. RALPH *stands in a daze. A familiar voice calls out.*

DEIGHTON: Ralphie! Ralph MacLean!

RALPH: Deighton. That you? Oh my brudder!

They embrace. DEIGHTON *helps* RALPH *over to a decent spot where he collapses in a heap.*

DEIGHTON: Look at you, Ralphie. You all right? Not hurt anywhere? I figured you were a goner. A goner for sure. Volunteering for the first danger mission to come down the pike—what were you thinking?

RALPH: Just doin' my job.

DEIGHTON: Well you can stop being a hero cuz our war's over.

Beat.

Hey. Where's Coop? You seen him?

RALPH: Japs killed him. He was hurt, but not that bad. They shot him like they were putting down a dog.

They grieve their lost friend for a beat, which is all they can afford.

DEIGHTON: I've seen worse. A lot worse. There's one guy in here. Big Jap we call the Kamloops Kid on account of he's from there. He's an interpreter, speaks perfect English. You see him, don't matter if he's a hundred feet away, put your head down and walk the other way. He hates us cuz of how he was treated back home. So he says.

DEIGHTON shakes his head.

He's sick in the head. I've seen him put lit cigarettes up a guy's nose. I've seen him kick another guy in the mouth till there was nothing left.

RALPH: We gotta get out of here. It's our job to get out of here.

DEIGHTON: Our job is staying alive.

RALPH scans the surroundings.

RALPH: What are all those guys doing on top of that wall? They got no pants on.

DEIGHTON: We don't got no latrines, so we hang our asses over the top, the boys that can still climb anyway. There's shit from a thousand men with the runs and every Chinaman the Japs killed all floating around in the harbour on the other side. Four guys went over last week trying to escape, somehow made it to shore before the Japs caught 'em, cut their heads off with a samurai sword. Since then, the Japs have a new rule: you escape, they kill everybody else in your barracks. So don't be getting any ideas, Ralphie.

RALPH: They can't treat prisoners like this.

DEIGHTON: The Japs don't take prisoners. They can do whatever they want. Come on. Let's get you a bowl and a spoon. Guard 'em with your life!

They exit.

Title: Hastings Park Livestock Building, Vancouver. 1942.

MITSUE and TOMI enter opposite, staring in horror at the filthy livestock pen they have been placed in. There are two crude wooden cots with bedrolls, soiled hay on the ground between them. A POLICE OFFICER makes his rounds. MITSUE calls out to him.

MITSUE: The Humane Society wouldn't let a cow stay in here. They wouldn't let a pig in this sty.

POLICE OFFICER: Good enough for you Japs.

TOMI: Do you have a shovel here? Something? So we can make clean?

POLICE OFFICER: You were to bring your own necessities with you.

MITSUE: Please. You can't expect us to stay here. No animal would. Stand in a pile of another animal's filth?

The POLICE OFFICER shrugs and starts off.

You can't just walk away. We were told our family would stay together. Where are our husbands? When can we see them? Answer me, please! I'm speaking to you!

TOMI: *Yoku keikan ni nattawa kono koshinuke yaro!* [*It's a wonder they let this spineless wonder in the police!*]

TOMI has made sure the POLICE OFFICER has heard. Her contemptuous tone is unmistakable. The POLICE OFFICER strides back and slams his baton into the wood of the livestock pen, inches from MITSUE *and* TOMI.

POLICE OFFICER: You will address me as "sir" or "officer."

(to TOMI*)* And you will either speak English or keep your mouth shut! Is that clear? *Is that clear?*

A standoff. The POLICE OFFICER *stalks off.*

TOMI: *Akireta. [Unbelievable.]*

MITSUE: You're right, Mama. I don't know how anyone, let alone a police officer, can even pretend they're doing what's right.

TOMI: They know they are not. We have to make best. Do what we can.

MITSUE: How?

TOMI assesses the situation. She finds a loose plank.

TOMI: Here. Help me pull. Be careful your hands.

They manage to pull the board loose.

Good. We can push dirty hay with this. Find clean hay to cover.

TOMI gets to work.

MITSUE: Mama, let me do it.

TOMI: No, no, my hands dirty already. You put suitcase up. Keep clothes clean and dry.

TOMI continues using the loose board to push the dirty hay into a corner. MITSUE *lifts a suitcase onto a cot. She is about to lift the second one up when she stops, horrified by what she sees.*

MITSUE: Mama . . .

TOMI: Hm? *Doshita no?* [*What's wrong?*]

MITSUE: *Mu . . . mushi ga . . . [Bugs . . .]*

TOMI: *Mushi?*

MITSUE swats at the suitcase and the bedroll beneath.

MITSUE: There're bugs, Mama! Bugs everywhere!

MITSUE jumps back, swatting at herself and groaning with revulsion. A wave of nausea hits her and she almost throws up. In the next instant, she breaks down and sobs. TOMI goes to comfort her.

I can't do this.

TOMI: Mitsue. *Shikkarishite. Ne?* [*Be strong.*] This not like you. We can make clean somehow. We have to keep going.

MITSUE: Mama. No. I think . . . I'm having a baby.

A beat.

TOMI: You think? Or you are sure?

MITSUE: I'm pretty sure.

TOMI: When?

MITSUE: October? November?

TOMI: Hideo know?

MITSUE shakes her head. TOMI considers, then smiles warmly.

Mitsue. *Ima wa taihen dakedo . . . [This is a bad time but . . .]*, baby is happy news. We will find Hideo-san and Papa and everything be okay. *Daijobu . . . Daijobu . . . [It's okay . . . It's okay . . .]*

Animation: the camps, the prisons, silhouettes of prisoners like lost souls in purgatory.

RALPH and MITSUE address the audience.

MITSUE: We still don't know where the men are.

RALPH: We're nowhere.

MITSUE: They could be in the next building. They could be on a ship to Japan.

RALPH: We don't exist anymore. We're alive, but only from one heartbeat to the next. One breath to the next . . .

The silhouettes periodically crumple to the ground and fade away.

MITSUE: The not knowing is exhausting. But God forbid you should lie down to sleep.

RALPH: As soon as you do, you're covered in fleas, bedbugs, every bloodsucking parasite known to man.

MITSUE: You can literally hear them, *kasa-kasa, kasa-kasa*. If you scratch or swat them, your hand comes away bloody. And there's only one sink and one shower for every fifty women.

RALPH: The stench. The stench is unbearable at first when it's something separate from you. But then you are the stench. The shit, the fever sweat, the vomit, the rotting bodies, that's all you. It's still unbearable. But now it's you.

MITSUE: We're at the mercy of every sickness you can get . . .

MITSUE: (*alternating with RALPH*)	**RALPH:** (*alternating with MITSUE*)
Measles, mumps, chicken pox,	Malaria, diphtheria, dysentery,
TB . . .	TB . . .

RALPH: Doesn't matter what. You're sick, is all. Sick and dying. Dying of thirst, dying of hunger, dying of everything.

MITSUE: We still don't know where the men are.

RALPH: We're nowhere. We're in a deep dark hole that goes on forever. When you're this lost to the world, you have to find one small thing to anchor you, to remind you of who you are.

MITSUE: You hold on to your dignity no matter what.

RALPH: Down here, the idea that you still have dignity—that's all. That's all.

SCENE 24

A blazing hot sun. The incessant drone of cicadas and other insects—the sonic manifestation of intolerable heat.

Title: Shamshuipo POW *Camp, Hong Kong. Summer 1942 (six months after capture).*

We find RALPH *and* DEIGHTON *huddled together in an embrace on the floor of their barracks.* DEIGHTON *is shivering and shaking despite the heat, his skin covered in sores.* RALPH *is trying to feed him some grey slop from a bowl.*

RALPH: You gotta eat, Deighton. You gotta eat. Try just a little. Try to get it down.

DEIGHTON: l can't . . . l can't swallow . . .

RALPH spoons a tiny smidgen of slop into DEIGHTON'S *mouth.* DEIGHTON *struggles mightily to swallow but cannot. He starts choking and collapses into* RALPH'S *arms.*

I'm gone, brudder . . . I'm gone . . . I'll see ya, Ralph . . . I'll see ya somewheres . . .

RALPH: No, Deighton . . .

RALPH looks around desperately.

Medic! Anyone! We need help here!

Captain MORTIMER *staggers over, barely alive himself.* RALPH *calls him over.*

Captain! Captain, can't you help? Do something, please. Anything.

MORTIMER: It's diphtheria. Bad. He needs penicillin. We don't have it.

MORTIMER examines RALPH's face.

How 'bout you, MacLean? Can you see outta this eye?

RALPH: A little.

MORTIMER: There's that hospital at Bowen Road the Japs make a show of for the Red Cross. Today's truck leaves any minute now. Be on it or you're done.

MORTIMER moves off.

RALPH: Did you hear that, Deighton? We're going to the hospital. I'm gonna get you there, brudder. Come on. We gotta move. We gotta move!

RALPH lifts DEIGHTON up and half drags him across the stage to a gate. We hear the sounds of a truck arriving off stage. Japanese guards and other POWs appear at the gate as the truck idles.

It's here! Let's go. We gotta go, Deighton!

RALPH does his best to help DEIGHTON to the gate. He cranes to get a look at the truck.

Don't worry. There's room for us. We're gonna make it.

At the gate a JAPANESE GUARD stops them and looks them over suspiciously.

Sumimasen. Truck? To the hospital. Me and him. There's room—

The JAPANESE GUARD *grabs* RALPH *and shoves him roughly past the gate toward the truck.* RALPH *stumbles, regains his footing, and turns to* DEIGHTON.

Come on, Deighton. You can do it. I'm here. Come on now.

DEIGHTON *shuffles forward. The* JAPANESE GUARD *stands in his way.*

DEIGHTON: Ralph?

RALPH: Hey! Let him through! He's real sick. He needs to go—

JAPANESE GUARD: Quiet!

(to DEIGHTON*) Omae wa dame da. [You're done.]*

He shoves DEIGHTON *away with his rifle.* DEIGHTON *falls back in a heap. The* JAPANESE GUARD *closes the gate.*

RALPH: NO! NO! There's room! There's room! Lemme help him! Lemme just—

JAPANESE GUARD: You! On truck! Go now!

The JAPANESE GUARD *roughly prods* RALPH *toward the truck.*

DEIGHTON: Ralphie . . . ?

RALPH: *(as he is forced off stage)* STOP! For the love of God! There's room! There's room, you bastards! There's room!

We hear a tailgate clang, a door slam. The truck shifts into drive and pulls away. In the dirt, DEIGHTON *smiles broadly.*

DEIGHTON: I'm open, boys . . . I'm wide open. Yeah yeah yeah
. . . Home free . . . Home free . . .

*JAPANESE GUARDS come and carry him away. MITSUE and TOMI
enter opposite. We hear HIDEO and YOSUKE's voices off stage . . .*

SCENE 25

HIDEO & YOSUKE: *(calling)* Mits? Tomi-san? *Kikoeruka?* Are you here? Sakamoto Mitsue! Oseki Tomi-san!

TOMI: Mitsue! It's Papa and Hideo-san! *(calling)* Papa, *kocchi kite!* [*Over here!*] *Hideo*-san!

MITSUE: Hideo? Here! Over here!

> *HIDEO and YOSUKE enter. MITSUE and TOMI rush over to them, overjoyed. They embrace as best they can through some slats of wood between them.*

Thank God! Hideo!

YOSUKE: *Oh yokkata yokkata. Tomi, daijoubu ka?* [*Good, good. Tomi, you're all right?*]

TOMI: *Un. Mitsue mo irushi . . .* [*Yes, I have Mitsue . . .*]

MITSUE: Are you together? Where are they keeping you?

HIDEO: Animal pen, same as here.

TOMI: And Pat? *Eichi wa?* [*What about Eichi?*]

YOSUKE: Pat sent to road camp. All single men have to go. I don't know where.

HIDEO: But good news is we can get out from here. We don't have to go to prison camp or be sent to Japan. There is a way we can work in Alberta. On a farm. Be together as family.

MITSUE: Be together?

TOMI: Us, too?

HIDEO: Yes. We can move same area. Have our own farmhouse. One house per family.

YOSUKE: Maybe Pat can join once we are there. We can work and make money.

MITSUE: Doing what? We've never worked on a farm.

YOSUKE: Work is work, Mitsue.

HIDEO: We will pick sugar beets. They use to make sugar, chemicals for rubber, explosives, many things. It's for the war effort, Mits. It's how we can show we are helping Canada.

YOSUKE: And they will pay thirty-three dollar per acre.

MITSUE: Is that good? An acre is . . .

   It's big.

HIDEO: I think together we can make one thousand dollar in one season.

MITSUE: We'd have to pick . . . thirty acres to do that.

YOSUKE: Mama and me still young. If Pat come, make big difference.

TOMI: *Doukana . . . [I don't know . . .] Mitsue ga . . . [Mitsue is . . .]*

YOSUKE: Mitsue strong. What choice we have? Here is prison. Work is freedom. *Shinpai surunayo, oi. [Hey, don't worry.]* Together we can do.

TOMI: If we can be together . . . okay.

YOSUKE: *Yoshi. Ganbaro. [Good. We'll give it our best.]*

HIDEO: Mits?

MITSUE: We'll be free, Hideo? Free to live?

HIDEO: Yes, Mits. This is our chance.

> *MITSUE, HIDEO, TOMI, and YOSUKE stand in tableau with their belongings as if on a train platform.*

> *Animation: We hear a train whistle and the clatter and rumble of the tracks. The landscape behind carries us from Vancouver across the Rockies to the prairies of Alberta.*

CONDUCTOR'S VOICE: Coaldale, Alberta! All Japanese are to disembark! Repeat! Coaldale! All Japs off the train!

> *In the background we see the confusion of the Coaldale train platform. There are crowds of Japanese families.*

FARMER'S VOICES: Taka-hashi family! Taka-hashis! You're with me! Fujitas? Which one of yous is Fujitas! Yoshimotos! Come with me!

> *On stage, our family search the crowd.*

HIDEO: *(consulting a sheet of paper)* Mr. Rutt? Is there a Mr. Rutt? Sakamoto family for Mr. Rutt!

> *MRS. RUTT enters.*

RUTT: I'm Rutt. You Sakamotos?

HIDEO: Yes. Hello. Very nice to meet you.

MITSUE: Nice to meet you, Mrs. Rutt. I'm—

RUTT: (*taking* HIDEO's *paper*) Lemme see that. (*re:* YOSUKE *and* TOMI) Who are these?

MITSUE: They're my parents.

RUTT: Are they on here? Didn't know there'd be elders.

Beat.

Well . . . as long as you understand everybody's gotta work. You're paying for your own food anyways.

As RUTT *continues, the background travels from the train station to a small farm.*

We're not a big farm. But all the beets gotta be outta the ground before the frost comes in October, sometimes end of September. It's good there's more of you than I expected.

We come to a small farmhouse . . .

TOMI: (*sotto*) This house? For all of us? It's so small . . .

We pass the house and approach a barn . . .

RUTT: Go on. Just past the barn there.

We arrive at an impossibly small crude wooden hut. A chicken coop.

MITSUE: This can't be. It's . . . it's a shed.

RUTT: It's a chicken coop.

HIDEO: Excuse me, but . . . this is not our house.

RUTT: You'll have to make the best of it. There's scrap lumber for repairs behind the barn. If you want any new materials, that comes out of your wages.

MITSUE: Make the best of it?

RUTT: There's a well at the end of that field there. Gotta boil the water cuz the animals use it. There's a couple brand new pails I bought for you in the coop there. I won't charge you for those.

TOMI: We came from livestock barn. And now this? Mrs. Rutt, we are not animals.

RUTT: We've had farmhands stay in there before. They were fine with it.

YOSUKE: (to HIDEO) Tondemo nai koto da na, oi. Shoyuusha wa dokonanda? [This is outrageous. Where is the owner?]

RUTT: Hey! None of that! You got something to say, speak English.

HIDEO: Excuse us. Where is owner of the farm?

RUTT: You have some nerve. Our men are at war.

MITSUE: Pardon us, he meant no offence. It's just . . . our men thought they'd be working for a Mister Rutt.

RUTT: My father-in-law. He passed not long ago.

MITSUE: I'm very sorry to hear that, Mrs. Rutt.

RUTT: Anyway, as I understand it this whole arrangement is voluntary. You either want to be here or you don't. Take it or leave it. And like I said, if you need anything, it comes out of your wages.

YOSUKE: *Ma, do-nika narusa. [Well, we'll figure it out.]*

HIDEO: (*off* RUTT*'s dirty look*) My father say "thank you."

RUTT *starts off.*

MITSUE: Mrs. Rutt. Maybe we can work together, help each other out . . .

RUTT: What do you think this is? A barn raising? You think I want you people working here? You think I want to be doing this?

MITSUE: I just thought—

RUTT *exits. The family continue to stare at the chicken coop and the empty surroundings. Suddenly* TOMI *sees something a short distance away—a sugar beet plant—and starts tugging and digging at it.* YOSUKE *joins her. After considerable effort, they succeed in pulling this one beet out of the ground.* YOSUKE *holds the beet up.*

YOSUKE: We will learn how to do. We will be best beet-picker family anyone ever see. *Ganbaro! [Let's give it our best!]*

Elsewhere, RALPH *enters dressed in industrial coveralls, hard hat and lunch-pail in hand.*

Title: Cominco, Calgary, Alberta. 1968.

Animation: Post-war Canadian industry. Men in hard hats. The industrial buildings and smokestacks of the Cominco fertilizer plant.

RALPH *approaches the gate of the facility,*

There are other workers milling about with their backs to RALPH, *smoking, talking, etc. When they turn around,* RALPH *sees they are all Japanese.*

RALPH *drops his things and runs, calling out in a panic.*

RALPH: Captain Mortimer! Mother? Phyllis . . . ? *Phyllis. I n*eed to come home . . . I'm . . . I . . .

He looks around.

I don't know . . . Phyllis? Where is this? PHYLLIS . . . !

PHYLLIS appears with a tall glass of ginger ale. We are in their bedroom in Calgary.

PHYLLIS: Ralph? Are you all right? May I come in?

RALPH *stares at her until he gets his bearings.*

RALPH: I'll be fine.

PHYLLIS: You had an episode at work.

RALPH: I got overheated is all.

PHYLLIS: Let's get you out of your work clothes. I brought you some Canada Dry.

PHYLLIS helps RALPH out of his boots, socks, and coveralls.

We don't need to go to the Hat this weekend. It's such a long drive. And in this heat?

RALPH drinks the ginger ale, empties the glass.

Oh my. Do you want some more? Want your Bible? Ralph?

RALPH: These Japanese folks . . . What do they do again?

PHYLLIS: Stan's parents? They have a few vegetable fields, I think. Odd jobs. And his father makes deliveries.

RALPH: So they're regular people. Not office types or anything.

PHYLLIS: I don't think so.

RALPH: I'll go back to work now. Put in half a shift.

PHYLLIS: You will not. We just got you undressed.

RALPH: Yeah, I'm going.

PHYLLIS: Ralph MacLean.

RALPH: I got a job to do. I know what that is. That gives me a purpose. I need that. What am I without it?

PHYLLIS: I'm calling you in sick.

RALPH: Phyllis!

She exits. He gets up to go after her. COOPER *and* DEIGHTON
*now enter, appearing to him as they were the last time he saw
them during the war: bloodied, covered in wounds and sores.*

No, fellas. Not today. Leave me alone.

COOPER: Ralph. Hold me up. Don't let me go.

DEIGHTON: Please, Ralphie. Help us.

RALPH: I gotta go to work, boys. What good am I if I don't work?

COOPER: What good are you if you don't help us, eh?

DEIGHTON: You left us, Ralph MacLean. We needed you and you
left us to die.

*RALPH clutches his head and shakes it from side to side, trying to
rid these visions from his brain.* COOPER *and* DEIGHTON *recede
into darkness. An angelic figure now appears in front of* RALPH: *a
young white nurse, a red cross in the centre of her nurse's cap.*

NURSE: Hello. How are you feeling? You're doing so much better
now. Do you know where you are?

RALPH: My feet are on fire. They're burning.

NURSE: That's the "electric feet." We think the barley and greens
you've been eating will help.

*She freezes suddenly as a JAPANESE GUARD emerges from the
shadows.*

JAPANESE GUARD: You. *Kocchi koi.* Come here.

*She cowers back. He moves close, smiling. He grabs her and
pulls her away into the darkness.*

RALPH: Hey. Bring her back. *Shitsurei. Sumimasen. Yamero! Yamero!* *[I'm sorry. Excuse me. Stop it! Stop it!]*

MORTIMER appears.

MORTIMER: Way to fight, MacLean. We didn't know if you'd make it.

RALPH: Captain Mortimer. Sir. I wanna go home. Can we just stop now and go home?

MORTIMER: Whoa now. Take it easy, son.

RALPH: Why can't we? Where even are we?

MORTIMER: This is Bowen Road Hospital. The truck, remember? You've been here three weeks. I got here a little while after you.

RALPH: Bowen Road? Are we in Canada? I saw a nurse. The Jap took her. Are the Japs in Canada?

MORTIMER: Shhh. Settle down now.

RALPH: Is Deighton here?

MORTIMER puts a heavy hand on RALPH's shoulder.

MORTIMER: Listen. Every crumb, every smear of food, every drop of water, put it in you. Once the Red Cross leaves, they're shutting this place down. We're being shipped out.

RALPH: Where we going?

MORTIMER: Going to fucking Japan.

There is an evocation of blazing sun and searing heat and . . .

Animation: The Prairies. Japanese families toiling in the Alberta sugar-beet fields.

MITSUE, HIDEO, TOMI, and YOSUKE are working under the blazing sun, all obviously exhausted. MITSUE gets up and addresses the audience. She is seven or eight months pregnant.

MITSUE: Those first summer months on the beet farm, we lived in Mrs. Rutt's chicken coop.

Well . . . we didn't exactly "live." We survived. Barely. We endured. Up at dawn, back at dusk, a sponge bath in a galvanized tub, a meal, then bed: Mama and Papa on one mattress, Hideo and I on the other, a sheet strung up between for a little privacy. Even in the summer the holes in the roof and gaps in the plank walls were an affront to our sense of ourselves. Papa and Hideo bought wood and tarpaper we couldn't afford to patch the holes. We did not earn thirty-three dollars per acre. Pat did not join us. He was in a prison work camp in Ontario because in addition to being young and single, he had a big mouth and an attitude. When the harvest season started in earnest, I just didn't think there was any way we could make it.

A long beat.

And I was right . . .

MITSUE heads back to the beet field but doubles over on the way.

Title: Coaldale, Alberta. Summer 1942.

HIDEO: Mits! You okay?

He rushes over with some water. She drinks a little but can't keep it down. TOMI *comes over. They help* MITSUE *to a shady spot with their supplies.*

TOMI: *Daijoubu-daijoubu.* [Okay, okay.] *Shikkarishite.* [Pull yourself together.]

MITSUE: I'm fine . . . It's just the morning sickness. The all-day-every-day-until-the-end kind.

TOMI: Ohhh, you got from me, Mitsue. I'm so sorry. *Gomen, ne.* When I have Eichi I have so bad, too. *Sukoshi yasuminasai.* Rest, okay? Almost lunch anyway.

(calls to YOSUKE*)* Papa! Break early!

YOSUKE: Twenty minutes! I finish this row.

YOSUKE continues working. TOMI starts unpacking their lunches. MITSUE lies back against HIDEO.

TOMI: *Kyo mo onigiri.* [Onigiri again today.] With extra salt. Inside is *fuki* [butterbur] we found.

HIDEO: Your *fuki* and extra salt is the best, Tomi-san. *Itadakimasu.* [Thank you for this food.]

TOMI digs out some containers from the ground.

TOMI: Oh, good, still little bit cool. Papa bury for us in the morning.

She calls to YOSUKE.

Papa! Come. *Mugicha ga mada sukoshi hieteru wa.* [The barley tea is still a bit cool.]

YOSUKE gets up. Dusts himself off. Wipes his brow. He winces suddenly. Did he get up too fast? He bends over with his hands on his knees. He collapses in on his left side, the left elbow going down to the knee. He shakes, staggers, then goes to the ground.

TOMI is getting the onigiri *and tea organized. HIDEO is busy eating. MITSUE is resting with her eyes closed. No one sees YOSUKE go down.*

HIDEO: *(eating)* Tomi-san, *oishii! [Delicious!]* Mits, you want some?

TOMI: *(finally looking up)* Papa? *Nani shiteruno . . . [What are you doing . . .]*

She realizes something is wrong.

Eh. Anata . . . ! [an affectionate "you" used by married women]

The others hear the alarm in her voice. They all rush over to YOSUKE.

Oto-san, doshimashita? Memae? [What happened? Are you dizzy?]

MITSUE: Papa? Papa, please . . . ! He needs a doctor, Hideo!

HIDEO: I'll get Mrs. Rutt.

HIDEO scans the horizon, then starts waving and yelling.

Mrs. Rutt! Help! We need help! Mrs. Rutt!

TOMI: *Anata . . . Okite . . . Okite hora . . . [Get up . . . Come on, get up . . .]*

TOMI lets out an awful wail.

MITSUE: Papa? No! Please, no . . .

HIDEO looks back to see MITSUE and TOMI weeping over YOSUKE's lifeless body. He knows it's no use. He joins them and . . .

Animation: YOSUKE's spirit gets on his fishing boat and casts off. He waves from the deck as he sails away . . .

*Animation: Another much larger vessel now looms into view.
It's a "hell ship," the* Manryu Maru, *a bulk cargo ship the
Japanese used to transport* POWs. *We see prisoners marched
onto the vessel, where they are forced to descend further and
further down into the depths of the cargo hold, packed in so
tightly there is literally no room for them all to lie down. The
hatch is shut, enclosing the prisoners in darkness.*

RALPH enters to address the audience.

RALPH: We called them "hell ships." And for good reason. Same
as anywhere, Japan had a labour shortage with all their able-bod-
ied men at war. So they shipped us POWs to Japan as a slave labour
force. Over a hundred thousand of us. For transport they used
unmarked cargo vessels. Dozens of them were sunk by Allied forces
who had no way of knowing these ships were full to the gunwales
with our own soldiers. From Hong Kong, three hundred of us were
packed into the hold of a ship designed for hauling coal. The Japs
didn't bother washing the coal dust out. We were packed worse
than sardines—there wasn't enough space for all of us to lay down
at the same time. Not that you exactly wanted to. There were no
toilets, no clean water, no light, no air. Hell ship?

He nods.

Only thing missing were the flames of damnation. Which could
come at any moment from an American plane, a torpedo. We were
down there in that darkness for seventeen days.

MITSUE enters.

MITSUE: Mrs. Rutt gave us a day off and we buried Papa in a small
graveyard down the road. What will we do now, Hideo and I

wondered. Try to find a farm with a more kindly owner? Go to one of the prison camps? How could that be worse? Surely they'll let us stay together? But when we got back to the chicken coop, Mama went straight back to the fields without a word and started picking beets. Up and down the rows she went, working until it got so dark we couldn't see her. We went out to talk to her, to ask her what she thought of going to a camp. "That is not what Papa wanted," she said. "Camp is prison. Work is freedom."

MITSUE rubs her pregnant belly.

Is work freedom for slaves? Will my baby be out here picking beets as soon as it can walk? Is this how caged birds feel?

As MITSUE exits, a lost voice is heard in the darkness.

VOICE: Send a torpedo . . . Send a torpedo . . .

RALPH: Seventeen days.

VOICE: Send a torpedo . . .

RALPH: It went on. Minute by minute. Hour after hour.

VOICE: Send a torpedo . . . Send a—

A slight commotion. Choking. Silence.

RALPH: Somebody nearby must've done him in. Had to.

Animation: A hatch is opened. Blinding light blazes down on the prisoners. They wail and moan like ghouls of the night recoiling from the sun. JAPANESE GUARDS start moving them toward the gates of a POW camp.

Title: Niigata 5-B POW Camp. September 1942.

RALPH and MORTIMER listen as an American officer, ADAMS,
addresses the new prisoners. RALPH is a shell, barely able
to stay upright. Elsewhere, Commandant KATO watches
imperiously.

ADAMS: If you're thinking things can't get worse being in Jap-land—
there'll be more food at least—you're wrong. And the guards here?
Bottom of the barrel. Any half-competent Jap is off fighting somewhere. Being here is a humiliation for these fuckers and they're
gonna take it out on you. They'll hit you for looking 'em in the eye.
They'll hit you for averting your gaze. They'll hit you for standing
up straight. They'll hit you for bowing too low. Treat 'em like a bear
in the woods, okay? Don't look 'em in the eye. Don't turn your back
either. And if one of 'em is on you, well, you best go limp and play
dead cuz he'll kill ya for fighting back.

MORTIMER starts off. ADAMS stops him, and they confer briefly.
MORTIMER reluctantly indicates RALPH and exits. ADAMS turns
to RALPH.

You. MacLean?

RALPH: Sir.

ADAMS: Adams. US Marines. I'm gonna give it to you straight. In
your condition, you won't survive a regular work detail. You won't
survive *not* working and getting half-rations. And you won't survive
the infirmary where they won't bother feeding you.

A beat.

Now. The camp commandant. Kah-toe. He likes to have a prisoner
serve him his meals, pour his whisky, listen to him fuck up the
English language. You'll get a bath. You'll get your full rations of
maggoty rice and bilge-water soup. And you'll be inside. Might give
you a chance to catch your breath, get your strength back.

RALPH: I don't want special treatment, sir.

ADAMS: Understand, MacLean, no one wants this job. This Kato character is on a dark road to nowhere. Especially when he's drinking. Whether or not you survive him depends on his mood. Your call.

ADAMS exits. RALPH mulls his options for a beat then heads up to KATO's office.

KATO: Name?

RALPH: MacLean, sir.

KATO: Makurane. Spell.

RALPH: Capital M, a-c, capital L, e-a-n.

KATO: Ho. English is strange. You learn Japanese: *Nippongo*. I say *tsu-ge* you pour whisky. I say *saga-re* you step back.

RALPH: *Hai.*

KATO: You are Christian?

RALPH: *Hai.*

KATO: You believe *Ehoba* God. *Iesu Kiristo.*

RALPH: *Hai.*

KATO: You believe God is good, love, all power. Can do anything. Is everywhere.

RALPH: *Hai.*

KATO: How? Why?

> *KATO makes a show of looking around. Indicates his quarters, the hell of the camp beyond.*

I believe Shinto. Religion of *Nippon*. Shinto, some god good, some god bad. I also believe *Bukkyo*, religion of Asia. Life is suffering. I think this is true. Christian God, not true.

Silence.

Macurane. I have scientific proof Christian God not true. If God is all good, all love, all power, why there is war?

RALPH: Men make war. Nations make war.

KATO: If Christian God is all power, he should stop war. Can God make prison he himself cannot escape?

RALPH: *(thinks hard)* Hai.

KATO: Not true. If he *can* make this prison and he *cannot escape*, he is not all power. If he *can* escape, he *cannot* make the prison. So, this is God paradox, teach to me by my father, philosophy professor. Very wise man.

RALPH: *Hai.*

KATO: So, Macurane. Why you are Christian? I prove to you your God not true.

RALPH: I believe . . . God could choose to make the prison. He could choose to escape.

KATO laughs. He gestures to his whisky glass.

KATO: *Saga-re.*

RALPH steps forward to pour. KATO suddenly backhands RALPH then grabs him by the collar and punches him hard in the face.

I said *saga-re*. Not *tsu-ge*. *Saga-re!* SAGA-RE!

RALPH: *Hai.*

> *RALPH staggers back as best he can.*

KATO: *Yoshi. Tsu-ge.*

> *RALPH fearfully steps forward and reaches for the whisky bottle. He pours. KATO slams it back.*

Mo ippai. Tsu-ge.

> *RALPH pours again.*

Thank you, Macurane.

> *RALPH bows. KATO smiles warmly.*

You see. I can *choose* to beat you. I can *choose* to kill you. Am I God?

RALPH: No.

KATO: No?

> *KATO draws a pistol and points it at RALPH's forehead. KATO laughs. We hear MITSUE's voice . . .*

SCENE 30

*MITSUE and TOMI are on their hands and knees picking beets.
MITSUE is struggling. HIDEO works on his own row a short distance away.*

MITSUE: Chinese Japanese, dirty knees, look at these . . . Chinese
Japanese, dirty knees, look at these . . .

TOMI: *(scolding)* Mitsue.

> *They work in silence for a beat. MITSUE starts singing "O
> Canada."*

Mitsue! I am working. Don't make worse.

> *MITSUE starts crying.*

*Guzu-guzu yamenasai! Mittomonai! [Quit snivelling! Aren't you
ashamed!]*

> *MITSUE has had enough. She sits in the dirt, unable to go on.
> TOMI catches sight of MITSUE's gold cross necklace.*

Jujika hazushinasai. [Take off that cross.]

MITSUE: *(reaching for it)* Eh?

TOMI: Take off.

MITSUE: Why?

> *TOMI grabs MITSUE and tries to rip the cross from her neck.*

Mama!

HIDEO rushes over and pulls TOMI from MITSUE.

HIDEO: Tomi-san! *Yamete-kudasai!* [*Please stop!*]

TOMI collects herself.

TOMI: *Sonna kudaranai mono.* [*Such a useless thing.*] Take off and throw away.

MITSUE: (*taking it off*) I'll take it off. But I won't throw it away.

TOMI: We are not Christian, Mitsue. This is not a Christian country.

TOMI stalks off. HIDEO comforts MITSUE.

HIDEO: *Daijobuka?* [*You okay?*]

MITSUE: No, I'm not okay. None of us are okay.

HIDEO: *Ma, ganbaro. Shikataganai daro.* [*Well, we'll do our best. Nothing else we can do.*]

MITSUE: No. Not *shikataganai*. Not *shikataganai*, Hideo.

HIDEO: *Do surette iyundayo?* [*What do you want me to do about it?*]

MITSUE: You could speak to me in English for starters.

HIDEO: *Tsukareta.* [*I'm tired.*]

MITSUE: You and my mother both? What's happening to us?

HIDEO: *Nani ittenda.* [*Whattaya talking about.*]

MITSUE: You say, *ganbaro. Ganbaro!* But you're not even trying anymore—

HIDEO: Not trying?

HIDEO explodes.

Ichinchi-jyu hataraiterudaro! [I work all day!] I work dark to dark! Dark in the morning, dark at night, every day, working, trying! *Trying!*

A beat.

I'm sorry, Mits. I am trying.

MITSUE: We're having a baby, Hideo. The bucket froze last night. It's only September.

HIDEO: How much money we have? You know?

MITSUE: Twenty-four dollars and fifty-three cents.

HIDEO: Twenty-four dollars. We work all summer, your father die, we have twenty-four dollars. Already we are borrowing against next year's crop.

MITSUE: Why? What's the point of staying here? There's no crop in the winter, no work. We'll just go deeper into debt, get sick . . . and worse. I am not raising a baby in a chicken coop. Not for a minute.

They sit in silence contemplating their options, of which there are none.

HIDEO: Put on your cross. Come with me.

MITSUE: What are we doing?

HIDEO: We're going to find a home.

He helps her up. She puts on her necklace as they cross to Mrs.
RUTT, who enters opposite.

You see us only as Japanese. But we are a family with baby coming.
We are good workers—we work hard for you. We ask for nothing.
We are Christian like you. We are all Canadian. We are more alike
with you than different. You would not survive winter in chicken
coop. Neither will we.

RUTT: You expect me to take you into my house? And what, sleep in
my dead father-in-law's bed?

HIDEO: You have space in your barn. Empty stalls with old farm
equipment. We will fix, clean, organize for you. In exchange, please
let us build small space for my wife and our baby.

RUTT: I can't afford to be buying you any lumber.

HIDEO: I understand. You can deduct from our wages.

RUTT: You can't have a fire in there. I don't want the barn burning down.

HIDEO: There is old stove. I will fix. Please, Mrs. Rutt.

RUTT considers but seems ill-inclined.

MITSUE: Blessed are the merciful, Mrs. Rutt. Blessed are the
peacemakers.

RUTT: Don't you speak the Gospel at me. I'm all alone here. Don't
you see that?

HIDEO: I understand.

HIDEO starts to back away.

MITSUE: I'm having a baby.

A beat as RUTT and MITSUE see the impossible situation they both are in.

RUTT: The barn could use some work. I could use a hand with it. Get started and if I like what I see, you can stay the winter.

Animation: Snow falls. We see the snow form numbers, which count off the years: 1942 . . . 1943 . . .

RALPH enters. He and MITSUE address the audience.

RALPH: Blessed are the poor in spirit . . .

MITSUE: Blessed are those who mourn . . .

RALPH: Blessed are the meek . . .

MITSUE: Blessed are those who hunger and thirst for righteousness. At last we had a home. Just a corner of Mrs. Rutt's barn, yes, but it was dry, the stove was warm, and my mother cleaned it as only a Japanese *obaachan* can. And it was ours. Her spirits improved a little when Ron was born, and it wasn't long before I was expecting again.

RALPH: Things improved for a while. Adams and Captain Mortimer said I was a good influence on Kato. His cruelty did mellow. For Christmas he even let us have some Red Cross packages he'd been hoarding—food beyond imagining—bully beef and sausages, sugar biscuits, condensed milk, chocolate. I got a letter from home. It was over a year old, but it was something. I must've read it fifty times a day.

MITSUE: We got a letter from Pat, as well as from other Celtic families who were in camps or on other farms. It was nice at first to get letters, but then most of the news inside was bad. The church in Celtic mysteriously burned down with all of the belongings our community had stored inside. In one fell swoop, our memories, the lives we had put on hold . . . all gone. "They are just things, Mitsue," Mama said. "Things. We can always work and get more." Can we? Family albums, heirlooms, wedding kimonos, baby clothes, school report cards . . . We lost all trace of our pre-war lives and of Celtic itself. What we had built there. Who we had been. How would we ever get that back?

MITSUE exits.

RALPH: At some point, the Japs couldn't hide anymore how badly things were going for them, and Kato was once again a danger to us. I've never been more afraid than I was then. When you see the end of the tunnel up ahead but you have to go through a madman to get there. And whether you make it or not—it's entirely up to him.

Animation: Snow falls again, this time over the Niigata POW camp. High in the sky we see an American B-class bomber. Its contrails and the falling snow counts off the years: 1944 . . . 1945 . . .

Title: Niigata 5-B POW Camp. February 1945.

Winter. We hear the cries and moans of someone in agony.
JAPANESE GUARDS march ADAMS in, arms behind his back,
tied to a heavy wooden stake. He is barefoot, wearing only
an undershirt and trousers. The guards erect the stake in the
ground. The prisoner struggles in agony against the cold,
trying to put one foot on top of the other. We see his toes are
black with frostbite. He can move about the stake a little,
but the rope prevents him from using his arms for warmth
or leaving his feet. Exhausted, he slumps forward and hangs,
Christlike, from his wrists.

MORTIMER restrains RALPH, who is trying to get to ADAMS.

RALPH: He saved us, Captain. I wouldn't be alive if not for him. We gotta cut him down, get him a blanket. For the love of God! He didn't do anything!

MORTIMER: They'll shoot you. They'll shoot you for so much as looking at him.

Beat.

It's the planes. Kato's spooked. If the Yanks can fly their bombers around here at will, they must have Guam, Saipan, maybe even Okinawa. They can bomb this whole godforsaken country.

RALPH: So . . . it's over. It's just a matter of time. We gotta save him then. We can't let him die.

MORTIMER: It's over, MacLean, but you gotta stay alive. That could be any one of us out there. Or all of us.

RALPH: No one else is dying. Not now. Not when we're this close.

MORTIMER: Listen. Japs might have a kill-all order.

RALPH: A what?

MORTIMER: Kill all prisoners. Adams talked about it—they've done it before. Wiped out whole camps when things went south on 'em. I need you to find out what you can from Kato.

RALPH: What am I supposed to do, say, "Excuse me, but do you have an order to kill all of us?"

MORTIMER: Just suss him out, MacLean. Get a sense of where his head is at. If he has the order and they come for us, we gotta be ready.

> *RALPH leaves and heads up to KATO's quarters. KATO is very drunk.*

KATO: *Tsu-ge.*

> *RALPH pours.*

You enjoy whisky, Macurane?

RALPH: Beer, occasionally. My father . . . drank himself to death.

KATO: Oh. My father same. Still alive, but . . .

> *KATO makes a drinking gesture.*

Too much.

> *A beat.*

Your father give land to you? Big farm?

RALPH: No.

KATO: No? Canada so big! So much land!

RALPH: I come from a small island.

KATO: Small island! Like Japan!

RALPH: Much smaller.

KATO: Smaller!

    KATO laughs.

When war is over, you and me, we are same.

RALPH: When . . . the war is over?

KATO: (*points to the sky*) Yes. Soon.

RALPH: I . . . hope to survive till then. All the men hope to survive.

KATO: Mm. Macurane father dead. But mother Macurane. So happy if you are able to come home from war.

RALPH: *Hai.*

KATO: Mother cooking always best. And mother smile when she give you your food.

    RALPH is overcome with emotion. He nods stiffly, trying to hold it in.

Tsu-ge.

    RALPH pours. KATO notices the emotion he's trying to hide.

You are thinking of home.

RALPH: *Hai.*

KATO suddenly pulls his pistol and points it in RALPH's face.

KATO: I can kill you regardless.

Silence.

So-daro! [Isn't that right?]

RALPH: *Hai.*

KATO: What can you offer me not to kill you.

RALPH: I . . . I have . . . nothing to offer. Nothing of value.

KATO: So if I spare your life, this is act of kindness. Compassion. Because I gain nothing.

RALPH: My gratitude. If you value kindness and compassion, I can offer you my gratitude.

KATO: Gratitude is to be expected. Therefore, no value.

KATO cocks the pistol. RALPH is paralyzed: anything he does could be a wrong move.

Tsu-ge.

RALPH pours. KATO drinks.

I have been good to you, Macurane.

RALPH: *Hai.*

KATO: Why you not offer me your friendship? Your loyalty?

RALPH: It . . . seemed presumptuous.

KATO: *Pre . . .* what? What is this word?

RALPH: I didn't want to . . . *assume* you would value these things.

KATO: But I do! I do!

> *KATO has trouble containing his grief as he aims his pistol at RALPH's face. At last he puts the gun away.*

I will spare you. I am too generous.

RALPH: *Arigato gozaimasu.*

KATO: *(sentimentally drunk)* You will see your home again. In Japan we say *furusato.* Hometown. Beautiful children song, *furusato.* But when I hear this, I am sad because *furusato* is small village with mountains, clean river, fish, and rabbit. But I am born Tokyo! So as a child I feel I have no *furusato.* This is very sad, Macurane. But what is more sad? To have no *furusato,* or to never see *furusato* again?

> *KATO waves RALPH off. RALPH exits. KATO starts singing the song "Furusato." Elsewhere MITSUE and TOMI enter with baskets of laundry. They, too, are singing "Furusato" and . . .*

Title: Coaldale, Alberta. Summer 1945.

The women start hanging their laundry on a line. MITSUE *has one baby strapped to her back and another one strapped to her front.*

KATO *is on his way off from the previous scene when . . .*

Animation: Pika-don! The blast of the atomic bomb.

It is not an event, of course, that affects KATO *in Niigata nor* MITSUE *and* TOMI *in Alberta. And yet it does affect them somehow. They sense something imperceptible.* KATO *exits.*

HIDEO *is now heard calling from the distance. His voice gets closer.*

HIDEO: Mits! Tomi-san!

TOMI: *A-re. Nanika attanokana?* [*Uh oh. Did something happen, I wonder?*]

HIDEO *races in, out of breath.*

MITSUE: Hideo? I'm afraid to ask.

HIDEO: Americans dropped atomic bomb.

MITSUE: Atomic?

HIDEO: *Genshi-bakudan.* One bomb destroy whole city. Hiroshima.

TOMI: *Masaka. Uso da.* [*As if. It's a lie.*]

HIDEO: Come. Come to delivery truck. News on *rajio.* Let's hurry.

He takes one of his babies from MITSUE.

MITSUE: Mama, are you coming?

TOMI: And leave wet laundry everywhere? I don't have time for nonsense.

HIDEO: Mits, come on.

MITSUE: *(to TOMI)* I'll be right back.

HIDEO and MITSUE exit. TOMI gets back to hanging laundry, but she is distraught. She starts weeping. She hangs a sheet and disappears behind it.

RALPH enters opposite in the half-light before dawn, confused by the emptiness around him.

RALPH: *Ohayo? Ohayogozaimasu . . . [Good morning.] Dareka! [Someone!]* This can't be. Am I dreaming? HEY! HEY!

RALPH laughs.

Wake up, boys. They're gone! They're gone!

MORTIMER enters, half-asleep.

MORTIMER: MacLean?

RALPH: The Japs are gone, sir. Every last one. I got up to take a leak, camp's deserted. They even left the gate open.

MORTIMER joins RALPH.

MORTIMER: Son of a bitch.

They rejoice, laughing and crying. Other soldiers appear, all cheering the end of the war.

Elsewhere: civilians run out to the streets in celebration.

ALL: The war's over! It's over! Thank the Lord! Oh sweet Jesus . . . IT'S OVER!

Animation: Jubilant throngs in the streets, waving newspapers with headlines declaring the end of the war: "Japs Surrender!" "War Over!" "Peace At Last!"

B-29s now fly over the Niigata POW camp. The bomb bays open and fill the sky with fifty-gallon drums floating down on parachutes.

On stage RALPH waits with his arms outstretched.

RALPH: We're saved, boys! Manna from heaven!

MORTIMER: Hey! Careful! Those are fifty-gallon drums coming in hard! Watch it, watch it now!

A drum lands near them and cracks open, spilling its contents. RALPH finds a Bible and cans of food.

RALPH: Jesus Murphy! Peaches! Canned peaches!

MORTIMER yells after some other soldiers.

MORTIMER: Get back, men! Out of the way! Let it land, goddammit!

Meanwhile, RALPH finds an opener and starts in on one of the cans. As he gorges himself on the sweet nectar, MORTIMER turns to watch him, amused.

Animation: A drum floats lazily down. A sudden gust of wind sends it spiralling and swinging through the air. The drum clips MORTIMER's skull, sending up a spray of red vapour.

When RALPH realizes what has happened, he is overcome by nausea and vomits. He catches his breath. He sees the Bible and picks it up.

RALPH: Why, Lord? Why am I spared?

He closes his eyes, riffles through the pages, and pokes his finger on a random verse. He reads it then gets up and rages at the Almighty.

This is it? Mark 11:25? This is all you have to say to me? After everything!

He exits, broken.

MITSUE enters and starts taking down the laundry from the previous scene. She's simultaneously jubilant, bitter, defiant, defeated . . .

MITSUE: The war is over! We're not the enemy anymore. We can go back home. Back to BC. Back to the river and the coast and the farms in the valley. Back to Powell Street. Back to Celtic. We'll come home from the internment camps and the Alberta beet farms, and we'll be together again. Families. A community. Like we used to be.

TOMI enters with an opened envelope, a stunned expression on her face.

Mama?

TOMI: Eighty-seven dollars.

MITSUE: What?

TOMI: The cheque for our property. Eighty-seven dollars. Papa's boats are worth ten times more. Just the boats! They sold everything for eighty-seven dollars?

MITSUE: We . . . always knew we'd have to start over. Rebuild. At least we'll be home. And we'll be free, Mama. We'll work. We'll work our way free—just like Papa wanted.

HIDEO enters with an envelope of his own.

Hideo? What have you heard? When will they let us back?

HIDEO: Mits. The War Measures Act. There is a new order.

MITSUE: The war is over.

HIDEO: War with Japan is over. War against us still going. We are not allowed on BC coast.

MITSUE: But that's our home. We're Canadian. *We're Canadian.*

HIDEO: We must stay east of Rocky Mountains. Or . . . government will pay us to leave Canada and go to Japan.

TOMI laughs bitterly.

TOMI: I will go then.

MITSUE: Mama, you will not.

TOMI: If I have to go by myself, I don't care. I will go.

MITSUE: You will not! Mama—!

TOMI exits.

Hideo. You're not seriously asking me to consider going to Japan? With Ron and Stan?

HIDEO: No, Mits, of course not. I looked into but—

MITSUE: You looked into it?

HIDEO: I have to consider all options. *All.* Insurance. Backup plan. I have to. I asked my parents. They say don't come. If *they* say that, you know it's bad.

A beat.

Look . . .

He pulls out a map from his jacket pocket and opens it.

This area Alberta. Two hours east from here. Medicine Hat. Most sunny land in Canada. Many crops will grow, not just sugar beet. Vegetables, corn, potatoes. We can rent land and a house. A real house. Stay in Canada. Start new life. Just like first *issei* who came to BC.

MITSUE: You're not a farmer. We are NOT farmers. The coast is our home. We're ocean people.

HIDEO: Sometimes I look at the prairie. It is like the ocean.

(off MITSUE's rejection) Just for now, Mits. Just until . . .

MITSUE: Until? What happens when they decide they want us out of Alberta, too? What then?

HIDEO: We can't worry about that. We have to take one step, one step, one step. Make a life here in Alberta until we can go back home to BC.

He gives her shoulders a reassuring squeeze. He exits.

MITSUE: *(looking up at the sky)* Until . . . Until . . . Until . . .

Animation: The years count off in the sky behind MITSUE with her every utterance of the word "until." 1946 . . . 1947 . . . 1948 . . .

SCENE 34

Title: Medicine Hat, Alberta. Spring 1949.

MITSUE pulls a letter from a pocket and reads it. We hear a baby off. HIDEO peeks from the wings.

HIDEO: Mits . . . Psst . . .

She goes to him. He hands her a swaddled baby (their daughter Glory).

She won't sleep. She needs her mama.

MITSUE: Come here, Glory. Come here, my baby.

The baby quiets in MITSUE's arms.

HIDEO: So . . . what you think? Some guys say wait two more weeks, make sure no more frost. But we can gain advantage if we plant now. Onion seed is cheap—

MITSUE: *(re: the letter in her hand)* Hideo.

HIDEO: What is that?

MITSUE: Another order.

HIDEO: *(bracing himself)* What now?

She strings him along for a beat. Then:

MITSUE: They're lifting the ban. As of April, we're allowed back in BC.

They do their best to hug and celebrate in silence because of the baby.

HIDEO: Okay. Let's . . . make sure we have a good year. Then next year, when we have money—

MITSUE: I need to go now, Hideo.

HIDEO: We can't afford. Three adults. The boys—

MITSUE: There's enough for one ticket. If you let me take Glory— she won't cost anything. Mama can cook for you and the boys while I'm away.

HIDEO: Mits? Why? Why you have to go now?

MITSUE: It's my home. The only home I've ever known. I want my children to grow up there. I want my mother back. I want her to smile again and laugh and be proud. I want my brother and all my memories and a chance at the life I thought we were going to have.

HIDEO: Mits . . . You're leaving me?

MITSUE: I'm not leaving you. I'm leaving . . . this . . .

HIDEO: But . . . there's nothing left there, Mits. After seven years?

MITSUE: There's *something*. There has to be. In Celtic. On Powell Street. I won't be the only one looking. There'll be others. We'll start all over again if we have to. Not just for me, Hideo—for us as a family. Can you see that? Please?

HIDEO: Mits . . . Are you coming back?

MITSUE: How can you even ask that? I love you.

They look at each other. HIDEO smiles.

HIDEO: *Sugao ga mieru.* I see the beauty of your honest face.

They kiss.

Animation: a train makes its way from the Prairies through the Rockies to the BC coast.

MITSUE is sitting on the train. A white woman takes a seat nearby. MITSUE looks up to see the woman staring at her.

WOMAN: What do you think you're looking at?

MITSUE: Excuse me, but you're the one looking at me.

WOMAN: What's wrong with that baby? It doesn't look right.

MITSUE: I beg your pardon. I'll thank you to leave us alone, please.

WOMAN: Don't you be telling me what to do. I can do what I want.

MITSUE: As can I. And I'd like not to be stared at by you.

WOMAN: Don't tell me what to do! You're an Oriental.

MITSUE: I'm Canadian.

WOMAN: Mind your place!

MITSUE: I'm Canadian.

WOMAN: No you are not. *I'm* Canadian.

MITSUE: I was born in Canada. In British Columbia—

WOMAN: Ohhh. You're a Jap. A Jap!

MITSUE: I was born—

WOMAN: I don't care where you were born. Don't you know by now we don't want you here. Your people attacked us. Your people killed good Canadian soldiers in a war *you started.*

MITSUE: My people? My people gave our homes, our families, our entire lives to Canada—

WOMAN: Shut your mouth!

For perhaps the first and only time, MITSUE loses her temper and raises her voice.

MITSUE: I will not! My people spent the war working. For Canada. Picking sugar beets for the war effort. I worked, do you understand? My whole family worked and everyone I know worked from dawn till dusk, grandparents down to little children. We worked. We worked. We picked acres and acres of beets and barely got paid enough to feed ourselves. And still we worked. As proud Canadians. *Canadians.* We worked! What did you do?

The WOMAN is outraged. She stalks out of the carriage in a huff. We hear laughter, a drunken male voice, and . . .

KATO stands in RALPH's bedroom in Calgary. RALPH sits on the bed in his undershirt and trousers.

KATO: What did *you* do, Macurane?

RALPH: I've been meaning to ask you.

KATO: Poured my whisky, shined my boots . . .

RALPH: Why me?

KATO: Why what?

RALPH: Why did you choose me? You could've picked someone who might've done something with their life.

KATO: What something? End war? Compose symphony? I did not choose you. You came to me.

RALPH: You spared me.

KATO: Surviving war is pure chance. Complete random. Look. There is a mirror behind you. Look inside that room in mirror, Macurane. In that room we are both dead.

RALPH looks behind him. When he turns back around KATO is gone. There is a soft knock on the door.

PHYLLIS: Ralph? May I come in?

RALPH: It's open.

PHYLLIS comes in and sits on the bed beside him.

PHYLLIS: It hurts me to see you like this, Ralph. And I just want to help you. What can I do?

RALPH: These are my demons, Phyllis. I don't think you can help.

PHYLLIS: That scares me.

A beat.

Sweetheart, we don't have to go to this dinner. I'll tell Di. She'll understand. We can go another time.

RALPH: I'm going.

He gets to his feet and rages at the darkness.

The war's over! IT'S OVER!

MITSUE, holding Glory, addresses the audience.

MITSUE: When I got off the train, I couldn't bring myself to go straight to Celtic. I decided to walk to Powell Street and went through Chinatown, which felt somehow normal and anonymous and safe. And then I walked by Hideo's parents' house and thought I saw a Japanese man on the steps. But another man came out and they started speaking in Cantonese. I didn't bother asking if I could have a look inside . . .

She walks.

I don't know what I expected to find when I got to Powell. Familiar faces, sounds, smells? The special music of *nikkei* English and Japanese. What I didn't expect was . . . emptiness. An emptiness I could see and feel from a block away. If you feel that way about Powell Street today, now you know why . . .

She walks again.

I headed downtown and got up the courage to get on the Granville bus. My heart was in my throat as we crossed the bridge. At the last second I got off at Broadway and walked up the street past the Stanley—a John Garfield movie called *We Were Strangers* was playing. It wasn't about us. And then . . .

MITSUE enters what used to be MRS. YAMAMOTO's dress shop.

Hello?

A gentleman, MR. ARCHIBALD, enters.

ARCHIBALD: May I help you?

MITSUE: Yes. I'm . . . looking for . . . Mrs. Yamamoto. This used to be her dress shop.

ARCHIBALD: Oh. Yes. I knew her. For several years. That's my tailor shop across the street.

MITSUE: Mr. Archibald. Do you . . . Would you happen to know . . . where she might be?

ARCHIBALD: Oh she's back in Japan.

MITSUE: You mean . . . After the war? She—

ARCHIBALD: Oh, no. Soon after she was interned. She wanted to be with family, and she managed to contact me. She made it very clear she wanted me to take over her shop if I could—she didn't want it auctioned. I paid her a very fair price. What I could afford. She was very happy and I was glad to be in a position to help.

MITSUE: Have you . . . been in touch with her since?

ARCHIBALD: I'm sorry, no. You . . . must know what part of the country she was from.

MITSUE nods.

I do hope she made out all right.

A beat.

You're Japanese Canadian?

MITSUE: Yes.

ARCHIBALD: Well. It's shameful what was done to you. Welcome back.

MITSUE: Thank you.

MITSUE gets back on the bus. She rides in silence. She gets off. She goes to the tree in the park in Celtic.

Hello, Miyoko. It's me, Mits . . . I . . . You . . . Oh, Miyoko . . .

She starts to speak several more times but cannot find the words for this communion. Finally:

This is my daughter, Glory . . .

She weeps. ICHIRO enters.

ICHIRO: Mits . . . ?

MITSUE: Ichiro . . . Oh my goodness, Ichiro . . .

ICHIRO: Are you okay? Why are you crying?

MITSUE: I just found out a good friend of mine was in Hiroshima.

ICHIRO nods. He gazes at the tree, the empty sky. MITSUE finally breaks the silence.

What are you doing back here?

ICHIRO: Same as you, I guess. Came back as soon as I could, just to see if . . . You know. Plus my parents had a box of valuables they buried in the garden.

MITSUE: Did you find them?

ICHIRO: That whole row of houses is gone. Tore 'em down, sold the lots for cheap to soldiers coming back from the war.

A beat.

That's a beautiful baby. Looks just like you.

MITSUE: Thank you. Glory. I have two sons also. They're with Hideo in Alberta. Do you . . . ?

ICHIRO: I'm not . . . I was in Slocan and the work camps out east.

MITSUE: But after the war? I thought for sure you were at McGill or U of T or . . .

ICHIRO: Yeah, they're pretty leery of Japanese in fields of "strategic importance." I wanted to go into engineering, so . . .

MITSUE: Well now the war's long gone you can go back to your studies.

ICHIRO: I'm going to Japan, Mits.

MITSUE: What?

ICHIRO: My dad's boat, our house, our car . . . We got this cheque in the mail—you know the one—I don't know if my dad's even cashed it yet. He's probably still staring at it. Anyway, my parents are done. They're going. And I can't let them go alone. They're so old, Mits. And they got nothing.

MITSUE: Oh, Ichiro . . .

ICHIRO: We did all we could, didn't we? We did everything we were supposed to do and then some. I'm glad we never got married, Mits. I'm glad you turned me down. If we were married and all this happened to us and I couldn't give you the life you wanted, it would've killed me. I would've thrown myself off a bridge or something . . . I'm sorry. I didn't mean to ruin your day. Anyway . . .

MITSUE: Ichiro . . . You can't go for good. This is your country—

ICHIRO: Look around, Mits. They don't want us here. They never did.

We find RALPH *in his bedroom, dressed for his road trip to Medicine Hat. He picks up a small suitcase and is about to leave when* DEIGHTON *and* COOPER *appear, ravaged by war.*

DEIGHTON: Where ya going, Ralph?

RALPH: I'm going to Medicine Hat. Having dinner with the family of a young man my daughter's sweet on.

COOPER: They're Japs, aren't they?

Silence.

Thought so.

DEIGHTON: Ralph? Is that true? You're leaving us for some Jap people?

RALPH: I'm not leaving you. I would never leave you.

COOPER: Yeah you would. You left us on the ground. Why didn't you pick us up? Why didn't you hold onto us? All we needed was a little help.

RALPH: I tried, Coop. I tried . . .

DEIGHTON: I coulda made it, Ralph. If you'd just taken my hand.

RALPH: I tried, fellas. You gotta believe me. I gave everything I had. I just wasn't strong enough . . .

He reaches out to them but collapses to his knees.

I'm sorry. Please forgive me. I can see your hand right there, Deighton. Right there. I'd take it now if I could bring you back. Oh what I'd give to bring you back . . . Coop. I feel you right there by my feet. Every day of my life. I just want to reach down and lift you up. And away we'd go. Back to the Magdalens, eh? The three of us. Running up the road to Sumarah's. Skating on the pond, all us Uproaders. I'll pass you the puck, Deighton. I'll pass you the puck all day. I'll see you back there one day, boys. But you gotta leave me now. I gotta live my life. And you gotta go back home. Please. I'm begging ya. Go home and rest in peace, my brudders. Rest in peace!

DEIGHTON and COOPER move to RALPH. They comfort him.

DEIGHTON: Hey. Where's that Bible of yours?

RALPH: I packed it.

COOPER: It's in the front zipper there. Get it.

RALPH gets the Bible out of his suitcase. The three of them sit on the bed. RALPH opens the Bible to the bookmarked page. COOPER closes his eyes and puts his finger down on the chosen passage.

The Gospel of Mark.

DEIGHTON: Read it for us, Ralphie.

RALPH: Mark 11, verse 25. "And when you stand praying, forgive, if you have anything against anyone, so that your Father also who is in heaven may forgive you your trespasses."

DEIGHTON: You gotta forgive yourself, Ralph. Me and Coop, we've been home this whole time.

COOPER: And we'll be waiting for ya when it's your time to come. Till then, go live your life for us. The life we couldn't.

DEIGHTON: Go in peace now, brudder. Go in peace.

DEIGHTON and COOPER exit. RALPH puts his Bible away, then goes to the phone and dials.

RALPH: Sweetheart, it's your dad. No, nothing's wrong, just about to hit the road. But listen, I have a favour to ask. When the baby's born, I'd like you to consider naming him Mark.

Beat.

I know you're not pregnant. I know. I'm just saying. When the time comes. Mark. Yes. I would like Mark to be the name of my grand-son. Will you think about it? Thank you. I'll see you in a few hours, sweetheart.

He picks up his suitcase and heads out. He is joined by PHYLLIS. STAN and DIANE enter. They move to the entrance of MITSUE's home, where MITSUE, HIDEO, and TOMI are waiting.

MITSUE: Welcome! Come in—

TOMI: Please take off shoes.

MITSUE: *Obaachan*—

PHYLLIS: Our shoes are very clean.

DIANE: *Mom*—

TOMI: Japanese house. Please take off.

MITSUE: *Obaachan. Shitade yukkuri yasundetara. Ne? [Why don't you take it easy downstairs. Okay?]*

STAN: Come on, *Obaachan*. You'll be bored up here.

TOMI: *Katteni shiyagare. [Do what you want.]*

    STAN *leads* TOMI *off.*

MITSUE: Old-timers! So set in their ways!

DIANE: (*to her parents*) But we do take our shoes off here.

PHYLLIS: (*to* MITSUE) We're very clean, I assure you.

DIANE: (*sotto*) Mother.

PHYLLIS: And Ralph is very sensitive about his feet.

MITSUE: I understand. And I have slippers for our special guests, if you don't mind. They're very comfortable.

A beat as MITSUE *holds out the slippers.*

RALPH: We don't mind, do we, Phyllis?

PHYLLIS: All right, I guess.

An awkward silence as RALPH *and* PHYLLIS *change from their shoes to the slippers.*

RALPH: Oh! These *are* better! Holy cow! I'm gonna wear these home!

He laughs. HIDEO *joins in. The women smile, the ice is broken slightly. They move to a small dining table off* MITSUE'S *kitchen.* HIDEO *gets* RALPH *and himself a beer.* STAN *returns and he and* DIANE *talk to* PHYLLIS *over* senbei *and almond choco. A kitchen timer goes off.*

MITSUE: Oh, excuse me!

MITSUE *checks on dinner, glad to have something to do. The others settle in around the table.*

HIDEO: So, Ralph, Phyllis, how did you meet?

RALPH: *(trying)* Well . . . I was on the train coming home from . . . the war . . . and . . . in Calgary I saw this pretty little thing at the station flirting with all the soldiers.

PHYLLIS: I was not flirting—I was cheering you on.

RALPH: Oh you were flirting so bad I knew I had to come back as soon as I could before some other guy got to you. So I went home, saw my ma, got some clean clothes, and came all the way back across the country just to take her out for a Sunday stroll. The rest is history.

PHYLLIS: Well I was waiting for you, Ralph MacLean—you're the only one I gave my number to. That came back for more, that is.

Genuine laughter. Finally.

RALPH: How 'bout you and your missus, Hideo? Is there a story there?

HIDEO: Very much same. I was working in logging camp, come to Vancouver every two weeks. Mits working in dress shop. Every two week I come and watch her through window. My friends all go to watch movie. I go to watch Mits through shop window. She is my movie!

MITSUE: *(from kitchen)* That must be why he never once took me out to the movies on a date!

More laughter.

RALPH: I hear ya, Hideo. I hear ya. We're two lucky dogs you and me.

They clink their beers. MITSUE enters with the barbecued salmon. STAN and DIANE help with the other dishes. TOMI has snuck back upstairs and spies from behind a corner.

MITSUE: Well it's really not much but I think we're finally ready to go . . .

STAN: Mr. MacLean, would you do us the honour of gracing this meal.

RALPH: *(sees TOMI)* The honour's all mine. But what about Grandma? Is she joining us?

STAN: *Obaachan?*

TOMI: No, no. No room for me.

RALPH: Oh we can always make room at a table. Move over there, Hideo.

Everyone shuffles to make room for TOMI. MITSUE is worried and goes to TOMI.

MITSUE: Mama . . . What do you want to do?

TOMI: *Ja . . . [Well . . .]* Maybe I will stay.

RALPH: Squeeze in here next to me. You don't mind, do you, Phyllis?

PHYLLIS: Are you going to behave yourself?

RALPH: *(to TOMI)* Shall I behave?

TOMI: We'll see.

RALPH laughs. Everyone enjoys the moment. STAN and DIANE initiate a joining of hands. RALPH collects his thoughts.

RALPH: Heavenly Father. We thank you for this food, this opportunity to join hands. We have all known hardship, Lord, and we do not take the bounty of this moment for granted. May we . . . surrender ourselves to your wisdom and know that you have gathered us here at Mitsue's table so our hearts may be nourished as surely as our bellies. Amen.

ALL: Amen.

DIANE: That was beautiful, Dad.

STAN: It really was.

STAN looks over at MITSUE, who is moved beyond words.

Well, shall we . . . ?

They pick up their forks and chopsticks, etc.

RALPH: Hang on, hang on. Mits, Hideo, is there a Japanese blessing before a meal?

HIDEO: Oh yes. Please.

HIDEO beckons for them all to join hands again. There is a beat of solemnity. Then:

Itadaki-maaaasu!!!

Laughter. They eat. RALPH *and* MITSUE *rise from the table and meet down stage.*

MITSUE: We spoke about the weather. Work. The aches and pains of growing older. The men speculated as to why Hideo's truck keeps back-firing.

RALPH: Phyllis enjoyed herself. Asked Mitsue for a recipe. The meal was not too salty for her in the least.

They return to the present of 1968.

I'm sorry if Phyllis and I came across as gruff and standoffish when we first arrived.

MITSUE: Oh please—not at all!

RALPH: I feel . . . very much at home here with you. I'm so glad to know you.

MITSUE: Thank you. That means everything to me.

HIDEO and PHYLLIS *join them.* TOMI *trails behind but steps forward to address* RALPH.

TOMI: Mr. MacLean. Thank you for your kindness. You are always welcome here.

RALPH: Well thank you all for your hospitality and an absolutely wonderful dinner. You know, Mits, you could charge good money—I'd gladly pay for your cooking. In fact, here's a little something . . .

He retrieves his wallet from his pocket. MITSUE *and* PHYLLIS *simultaneously slap* RALPH *on the arm.*

MITSUE: Ralph MacLean!   **PHYLLIS:** Oh stop it!

MITSUE: Seriously though, please stop by whenever you're in the Hat. It was so lovely to meet you both. And such an honour, Ralph.

HIDEO: Yes. Thank you. *Thank you.*

RALPH: You know . . . I fought over there for two and a half weeks. I spent the rest of the war just trying to stay alive. You folks fought for years and years. The honour's all mine.

RALPH throws a glance at STAN *and* DIANE *canoodling in the kitchen.*

I reckon we were all fighting for the same thing. Looks like it was worth it.

They all turn to the lovebirds. The Guess Who's "These Eyes" is playing on the radio. DIANE *cranks it. She takes* STAN's *hands in hers. They dance.*

We see the Grindstone boys on their frozen pond, MIYOKO *floating in the sky, and* YOSUKE *waving from the deck of his boat.*

MITSUE, RALPH, HIDEO, and PHYLLIS *turn out toward the audience and the promise of the future.*

The end.

BIOGRAPHIES

MITSUE SAKAMOTO

After the war, Mitsue never lived in BC again. She lived in the same house in Medicine Hat for sixty-seven years, and in her modest kitchen she fed many of the musicians her son Ron promoted over the years, including the Guess Who, Murray McLauchlan, Nitty Gritty Dirt Band, Bruce Cockburn, and many others. She passed away in 2014 at the age of ninety-three.

RALPH MACLEAN

Ralph settled in Calgary after the war, worked for Cominco for forty years, and lived there for the rest of his life. A decorated war veteran, he received the Queen's Diamond Jubilee Medal in 2012. At the time of his death in March 2020 at the age of ninety-seven, he was one of the last surviving Canadian soldiers who fought in Hong Kong. Though he lost his eyesight due to his wartime illnesses, he remained as vibrant and lucid as ever until the end.

STAN SAKAMOTO

An entrepreneur and lifelong community leader in Medicine Hat, Stan is a past director of the Medicine Hat Rotary Club and a former trustee of the Medicine Hat Museum and Art Gallery. In 2016 he ran for the federal Liberals in the riding of Medicine Hat–Cardston–Warner and, while he was not victorious, he gained more votes in the riding than any other Liberal candidate in history.

DIANE MACLEAN

Diane married Stan Sakamoto in 1973. Their sons Mark and Daniel were born in 1977 and 1980. After Diane and Stan divorced in 1985, Diane fell into alcoholism and substance abuse and spent the last years of her life in Medicine Hat's Cecil Hotel. She passed away in 2001 at the age of fifty-three.

RON SAKAMOTO

A legend in the country music industry, Ron was instrumental in launching the careers of Jerry Reed, Keith Urban, Shania Twain, and countless other stars. After Ron received the Canadian Country Music Association Promoter of the Year Award for seventeen consecutive years, the award was named after him. He was inducted into the Canadian Country Music Hall of Fame in 2014.

CAMP COMMANDANT TETSUTARO KATO

Kato was sentenced to death for war crimes, but his influential family was able to have his sentence commuted. He was released for good behaviour in 1952. He went on to write the war crimes apologia *I Want to Be a Shellfish*. The novel has spawned three film adaptations, most notably by Shinobu Hashimoto, writer of the Akira Kurosawa classics *Rashomon, Ikiru,* and *The Seven Samurai*.

ILLUSTRATIONS

Cover: *Forgiveness Montage*. Digital still of animation (charcoal and graphite on paper, pen, and watercolour), Cindy Mochizuki, 2022.

Pages 16–17: *Pre-war Celtic Cannery*. Digital still of animation (sumi on rice paper, pen, and watercolour), Cindy Mochizuki, 2022.

Pages 28–29: *Prairie Boys to Maritime Boys, The Hockey Sequence*. Digital still of animation (charcoal and graphite on paper), Cindy Mochizuki, 2022.

Pages 36–37: *Women Doing Laundry / Pre-war Celtic Cannery*. Digital still of animation (sumi on rice paper, pen, and watercolour), Cindy Mochizuki, 2022.

Pages 60–61: *Mighty Oak & the Ghost of Miyoko*. Digital still of animation (watercolour, pen, graphite, and rotoscope), Cindy Mochizuki, 2022.

Pages 92–93: *Rounding up Japanese Canadian Fishing Boats on the Fraser River*. Digital still of animation (sumi ink on rice paper and pen), Cindy Mochizuki, 2022. This illustration references the archival photograph "Japanese-Canadian Fishing Boats Seized at Annieville." Image C-07293, courtesy of the Royal BC Museum and Archives.

Pages 98–99: *War Scenes, R. MacLean*. Digital still of animation (charcoal, ink, and graphite on paper), Cindy Mochizuki, 2022.

Pages 126–127: *Shamshuipo POW Camp, R. MacLean*. Digital still of animation (charcoal and graphite on paper), Cindy Mochizuki, 2022.

Pages 144–145: *Sugar Beets*. Digital still of animation (watercolour and pen), Cindy Mochizuki, 2022.

Pages 178–179: *Train to the Prairies.* Digital still of animation (watercolour and pen), Cindy Mochizuki, 2022.

Pages 192–193: *Mitsue Sakamoto's Kitchen.* Digital still of animation (watercolour and pen), Cindy Mochizuki, 2022.

ACKNOWLEDGEMENTS

I cannot help but feel overwhelming gratitude for all the support this play has received, much of it through the height of the COVID-19 pandemic. None of this could have happened, of course, without the trust and kindness extended to me by Mark Sakamoto and his family: his uncles Stan and Ron, his aunt Glory, his brother Daniel, and, last but not least, Ralph MacLean himself, who I had the immense pleasure of meeting and interviewing before he passed away in 2020 at the age of ninety-seven.

The work of creating a play of this scale and ambition could also not have been done without the generous and steadfast support of virtually every resource available in the Canadian theatre ecology. From the word go, both the Arts Club and Theatre Calgary were unwavering in their belief that this play would be produced. The Banff Centre Playwrights Lab provided the time, space, and resources for me to complete the first draft. And an immensely important grant from the National Creation Fund allowed the design team to integrate animation by artist Cindy Mochizuki into the overall concept.

I am forever grateful to the Sakamoto family, Theatre Calgary Artistic Director Stafford Arima, Arts Club Artistic Director Ashlie Corcoran, dramaturg Stephen Drover, and to all the actors, theatre artists, and administrators who have helped to create this script and bring it to fruition. Additionally, I want to acknowledge some unsung heroes who have been essential not only to the development of *Forgiveness* but to my development as a playwright. First, Colin Rivers, my agent at Marquis Literary. Take a moment to imagine all the personalities and organizations who had to come together to create a show of this size and complexity. Colin played an indispensable role in making all of that happen as smoothly as it did. Second, Brian Quirt, director of the Banff Playwrights Lab. It is because of Brian's belief in me and his support of my ambitions that I could even dare to conceive of a play as large as *Forgiveness*. Finally, the Arts Club's Silver Commissions program. *Forgiveness* is my second Silver Commission—I was also a recipient in the inaugural cohort of playwrights in 2010. As you can appreciate, the impact of a Silver Commission goes far beyond the financial support. It is an affirmation that gives a writer the confidence and freedom to dream.

The phrase "it takes a village" comes to mind as I reflect on how *Forgiveness* was created. I hope all involved share in my pride at what we have accomplished.